SiMPLE
CHURCH

Other Books by Thom S. Rainer

We Want You Here
Who Moved My Pulpit?
I Will
Autopsy of a Deceased Church
I Am a Church Member
Transformational Church*
Simple Life*
Essential Church*
Vibrant Church*
Raising Dad*
Simple Church*
The Unexpected Journey
Breakout Churches
The Unchurched Next Door
Surprising Insights from the Unchurched
Eating the Elephant (revised edition)+
High Expectations
The EveryChurch Guide to Growth+
The Bridger Generation
Effective Evangelistic Churches
The Church Growth Encyclopedia +
Experiencing Personal Revival*
Giant Awakenings
Biblical Standards for Evangelists*
Eating the Elephant
The Book of Church Growth
Evangelism in the Twenty-First Century+

*Coauthor
+Editor

RETURNING TO GOD'S PROCESS FOR MAKING DISCIPLES

SiMPLE CHURCH

THOM S. RAiNER
& ERIC GEiGER

B&H
PUBLISHING GROUP
NASHVILLE, TENNESSEE

ISBN: 978-0-8054-4799-6

Published by B&H Publishing Group,
Nashville, Tennessee

Dewey Decimal Classification: 254
Subject Heading: CHURCH ADMINISTRATION \
CHURCH \ CHURCH GROWTH

10 11 12 13 14 15 • 22 21 20 19 18

From Thom:
To Nellie Jo
My love
My life
My heroine

From Eric:
Kaye, I dedicate this book to you.
Your relationship with God inspires me.
Your support and encouragement motivate me.
And your love brings me joy.

Contents

Acknowledgments

I have been a student of the American church for over twenty years. Though I realize I have only begun to understand this God-given institution, in some ways it seems as if I have studied it from every possible angle. Still I knew something was missing.

A couple of years ago, a young man with lots of energy came into my office to show me some research he had done. He couldn't sit still. Such is his nature, but even more so on this occasion. He was tremendously excited about the fruit of his research to this point.

Simply stated, he found that the healthiest churches in America tended to have a simple process for making disciples. They had clarity about the process. They moved Christians intentionally through the process. They were focused on the elements of the process. And they aligned their entire congregation to this process.

The simple church was discovered.

Eric Geiger was that young man, then a twenty-something but now an aging old man of thirty. His research was sound. His discoveries were on target.

We did further research, and the results were confirmed with even greater certainty.

I am grateful to Eric for his intellect, his enthusiasm, his persistence, and his humility as the "old man" (me!) offered guidance and a few suggestions for improvements.

Eric and I wrote this book in the first-person plural for easy flow. But we also note when we are speaking specifically about either one of us.

My gratitude also extends to my family at LifeWay Christian Resources, where I serve as president. The men and women who are part of this family are some of the greatest and smartest Christians I know.

Thanks also to Ken Stephens, the president of Broadman & Holman (B&H), for the opportunity to begin a new series of works with B&H, among which this book is the first. Ken's constant encouragement and dry sense of humor are always sources of joy for me.

How can I say thank you to my great family? In every book I write, you see me talk about my sons: Sam, Art, and Jess. One person recently asked me if these young men could possibly be as great as I describe. The fact of the matter is that I cannot overstate how wonderful they are. Every person who knows them agrees with me.

Of course, the object of deepest love among all of us in the Rainer family is Nellie Jo. Wife and mother *summa cum laude.* Isn't life great, Doll? Isn't LifeWay a great place? Isn't Nashville a great place to live? I love you so very much, and I love traveling on this journey called life with you. The best is yet to come.

—Thom Rainer

It has been said that it takes a community to raise a child. Well, it also takes one to write a book. I am eternally grateful to God for the community of people He has placed in my life.

I thank Thom for taking me on this journey. There is a lot of talk about investing in the next generation of leaders. Some would say at age thirty, I am a part of that next generation. Thom has lived that sermon. Thank you, Dr. Rainer, for believing in me and partnering with me on this project.

I thank all those who invested hours in the research phase of this project. I thank the hundreds of church leaders who participated with candor and honesty. Thank you, Dr. Paulette Johnson, for your statistical expertise. Thank you, LifeWay, for running the sample for phase one of the project. Thank you Bette Spellerberg, Stuart Swicegood, and Russ Kreuter, for making initial contact with church leaders.

I thank Dr. Rick Blackwood, my pastor, leader, friend, and mentor. Thank you, Rick, for giving me the opportunity to serve you and Christ Fellowship, Miami. The laughs, prayers, joys, and frustrations we have shared together have been rich and rewarding.

I thank the staff at Christ Fellowship. We are reminded constantly of God's grace and goodness. Not only do we get to serve Jesus and our great church, we also get to serve together. I pray we will continue to enjoy the ride together.

I thank the people of Christ Fellowship, Miami. I pray we will continue to push the movement of the gospel forward. Being a part of this church is awesome!

I thank Broadman & Holman for all the energy and time they poured into this project. When I first met Ken Stephens, the president, he said, "Welcome to our family." I felt like I was in a scene from *The Godfather*. I almost tried to kiss his ring. Almost. It was a great moment, and I hope there will be many more.

I thank the following leaders with whom I have had the honor to serve or study under: Jerry Key, Dr. Michael Hawley, Ben Wasson, Chuck Allen, Dr. Terry Fields, Dr. Dino Senesi, and Dr. Brad Waggoner. I am blessed because of your investment in me. I hope you see some fruit from your labor.

I thank my parents and brother. In the midst of enormous change, you have been constant. Even when I was far from God, you loved me. Your continual encouragement has supported me for years.

I thank my wife, Kaye. I am so thankful for you. I love you and I like you. You are the most tangible expression of God's grace in my life. Difficult days are much more bearable with you. Great days are much more exciting with you.

Most of all, I thank Jesus. I present this work to You as an offering to be used for Your glory.

—Eric Geiger

PART 1

Simple Revolution

ONE

The Simple Revolution Has Begun

Out of complexity, find simplicity.
~ ALBERT EINSTEIN

Relax. This book is not about another church model. If you are a church leader, you have been exposed to plenty of models. Most of them are on your shelf. Or worse, you have blended a bunch of models into one schizophrenic plan. If that is the case, neither you nor the people in your church are really sure what your church is all about. We see it all the time.

Go ahead, let down your guard. No new program is going to be pushed. There will be nothing new to add to your calendar. If anything, you will be encouraged to eliminate some things, to streamline. This book will help you design a simple process of discipleship in your church. It will help you implement the model you have chosen. It will help you simplify.

Keep your eyes on the words at the beginning of each chapter. Four simple words. Clarity. Movement. Alignment. Focus. Those four words will speak volumes before we conclude the book.

After hundreds of consultations with local churches and a significant research project, we have concluded that church leaders need to simplify. They are constantly asking, "How can we make all this work? How can we put all the pieces together?" Many of the church leaders we talk to are seeking an escape from the not-so-simple life.

The Not So Simple Life

Pastor Rush is on his way home from a conference on church ministry. He loved the time away, the challenging messages, and the extended times of prayer and worship. But he hates how he feels right now. The conference notebook sits on his lap filled with all that he learned and all that he wants to do. He wants to open it, but he can't. He wants to think about the future, but his mind is filled with the details surrounding the rest of this week.

As the plane takes off, he only feels the weight of the responsibilities that await him. Somewhere between ten thousand and thirty thousand feet, he puts the notebook (and his dreams) in his bag.

It is Wednesday afternoon. He feels a little guilty not being at the weekly visitation program last night. He feels more guilty for enjoying the night off. The Tuesday night visitation program was his baby, his paramount program, when he came to the church several years ago. It soon became the passion of many people in the church. He is grateful those people caught his passion and feels like a traitor for resenting the additional night away from home.

Tonight, he has to (wishes he wanted to) lead the prayer meeting at church. He tells himself he will share something God taught him in a personal devotion. By doing so he will have time to return some phone calls before the prayer meeting.

Experience tells him the messages on his desk and the e-mails on his computer will be many. He knows they are already there.

The financial team is meeting after the prayer meeting, so he will not be home until after 9:00. He does not lead the meeting, but he needs to be there. Hopefully his kids will still be awake when he gets home.

Tomorrow morning he is having breakfast with one of the men on the church board. He does not know what it is about, but he thinks it will only add more to his mounting list of responsibilities.

Then there is a staff meeting and maybe some hospital visits. Tomorrow night he and his wife are in a small group. He has recently encouraged everyone in the church to be in a small group, and he wants to lead by example. He genuinely loves the group when he gets there, and he wishes it did not feel burdensome. He asked each staff person to be in a small group and prays they don't feel the same way he does right now.

He has little work done on his message for the upcoming Sunday morning worship services. He is in the middle of a series on relationships. He taught on relating to your spouse last week, and he longs to live out some of the practical principles he shared: date nights, picnics, and so forth.

He wants to make that happen in some way this week. Friday night could work. He commits to pass on the invitation to attend one of the local high school sporting events. He knows that will disappoint one of the board members who has encouraged him to be more visible in the community.

Saturday afternoon, after his son's ball game, he will spend much of the day on his message. It looks like another "Saturday night special" is in store for the Sunday morning crowd.

This weekend he is going to speak on relating to lost neighbors. He wishes he had some personal stories to share, but life has just been so busy lately. He thinks of all the times he has pulled into the garage after late nights at church or church-related activities. He hasn't met the new couple two doors down. He tells himself they just moved in a few weeks ago but then remembers it was six months ago, at least.

He knows that if he is not relating to his neighbors and inviting them to Christ and to church, he cannot ask his congregation to do so. He wrestles with changing his message, but he has already announced what he is going to preach. He shakes his head and slumps a little lower in the seat.

He is tempted to witness to the person sitting next to him on the plane just to get a personal story for his message—nothing like a good airplane story to get a crowd going. He rebukes himself for the improper motivation. The passenger is asleep anyway. Must be nice.

Pastor Rush reaches back into his bag. He pushes the conference notebook aside and grabs a legal pad.

He has the weekly staff meeting after his breakfast appointment. This will be the only time he has to prepare for it. He decides to keep it brief, jotting down only a few items to discuss. He knows there are some staff issues that need to be dealt with, but he does not have the time or emotional energy to raise them.

He begins to think about his message for Sunday night (which is different from Sunday morning). He has taken some criticism lately for the quality of his Sunday night messages. He understands why. They have been underdeveloped. He is trying to work on them earlier in the week, taking some of the time away from the Sunday morning message preparation.

This Sunday night there is a neighborhood block party. His wife will go while he is at church. He thinks, *At least one of us knows our neighbors.* Of course, people will wonder why she was not at church. The tension is mounting. He slumps deeper into the seat.

He knows there has to be a better way. He knows it and continually admits it to himself and the Lord. But there is no time to discover *it* (whatever *it* may be), much less time to put *it* into action.

Like other conferences, Pastor Rush was impressed but is coming home almost depressed.

During these times, Pastor Rush has disciplined himself to remember his calling into ministry. When he was in his early twenties, he committed his life to vocational ministry. He mentally goes back to those days when he wrestled with his career path.

God had given him an unquenchable passion for the church, for the Word, and for people. He knew God had set him apart to serve the church. He still does. He still has a deep burden. The nagging in his heart to make disciples through the ministry of the local church is still there. That conviction has not wavered, only grown. But he knows so many things have been placed beside it, even on top of it.

Yet, he is in this for people.

At thirty thousand feet Pastor Rush is thinking of people in his church. He is praying and thinking. Some tough questions are emerging. Are the people in his church being transformed? Is his church making real disciples, the kind of disciples Jesus made? Or is everyone just busy?

He glances over at the sleeping passenger next to him. On his lap is the airline's magazine, and it is opened to a full-page advertisement for a popular media device. The top of the advertisement says *Simple.* Out of curiosity Pastor Rush pulls the same magazine out of the seat pocket in front of him. He finds the page to further examine the advertisement. It is interesting. He snickers.

Simple sure sounds good.

The Revolution

Simple is in.

Complexity is out. Out of style at least.

Ironically people are hungry for simple because the world has become much more complex. The amount of information accessible to us is continually increasing. The ability to interact with the entire world is now possible. Technology is consistently advancing at a rapid pace.

The result is a complicated world with complex and busy lives. And, in the midst of complexity, people want to find simplicity. They long for it, seek it, pay for it, even dream of it. Simple is in. Simple works. People respond to simple.

The simple revolution has begun.

Apple knows this.

They are pioneers of simple. They are a part of the revolution against complexity, pushing it forward on the technological front. Pick up an iPod and find one big button. Connect it to your Apple desktop, and music automatically downloads. Plug your printer cable into the USB port, and you are ready to go. "Plug and play," the mantra of a computer generation hungry for simple.

Even Apple's graphic design is simple. Look at the logo. An apple with one color has replaced the former multicolored apple. Their artwork on their products and in their stores is subtle. Their cultlike followers are vocal missionaries to the simplicity they offer. If you know someone with an Apple, you know what we mean. You have been prodded to join Apple's part in the simple revolution.

The iPod is a case study in action. If you are unfamiliar with an iPod, it's a portable music or video device that can be listened to with headphones or in a vehicle. It is the symbol of the present generation and is simpler than any eight-track, cassette player, or CD player. In an amazing coup that other companies are admittedly mimicking, Apple was able to take advanced technology and make it simple.

The outward design has only one circular button. It has four touch points surrounding the circle and one touch point in the middle, but it looks like one button. The iPod is more expensive and offers less performance than many of the devices sold by competitors, but it dominates the market. It is simple, and people respond to it.

The iMac is further proof. The iMac is Apple's version of a desktop computer. The attraction is that all the components of a computer are consolidated into one. The monitor contains the central processing unit, the speakers, the network and USB ports, and the CD-ROM. It comes in a single box with a keyboard and mouse. This simplicity makes the buying decision easy. There is one choice.

It is simple to assemble because of the few parts. Since Apple makes the software that comes with the iMac, there is one number to call if something goes wrong. One decision. One box. One contact. One price. Simple.

Google knows this.

Google is one of the fastest-growing companies in American history. It has made sophisticated technology behind Internet searching simple and speedy to users. The popularity of

Google has skyrocketed as Web users are flocking to use the search engine. People love and respond to the simple look of Google's search engine. Perhaps as much as 75 percent of all Web searches are done on Google. They are in clear command of the search market. For Google (and its investors), the simple revolution has been very rewarding.

The amount of white space on their home page screams simplicity. Click on google.com and only twenty to forty words are found on their home page. That's it. It is simple taken to a whole new level. If *simple supersized* were not an oxymoron, we would use it here. Compare Google's look to other search engines such as YAHOO! or MSN where users are confronted with hundreds of words on the opening page.

Google keeps its search page simple for the sake of the user. The philosophy behind the simplicity is that users are unable to effectively process too much information, that too much information is slow and cumbersome. Google believes users should not be assaulted with information that is not relevant or applicable to them.[1]

Graphic designers know this.

Graphic art has reacted toward the complexity and clutter of the postmodern era by embracing what some have called "the new simplicity."[2] Glance at some of the top graphic design magazines such as *I.D.* or *How*, and you will see hints of the simple revolution.

Or just take a look at simple revolutionary John Maeda, a leader in the graphic world. Maeda is a professor of design at MIT in Cambridge, Massachusetts. In 1999, *Esquire* magazine recognized him as one of the twenty-one most important people for the twenty-first century. He is also the 2001 recipient of the United States' highest career honor for design, the

National Design Award, and Japan's highest career honor, the Mainichi Design Prize.

Not only is Maeda one of the world's most renowned graphic designers; he is also an advocate of simple. He codirects SIMPLICITY, an experimental research program at the Media Lab at MIT. The research is designed to develop technology that is simple to understand and operate. The goal of the project is to help users break free from the intimidating complexity and information overload of modern technology. It is a funded revolt against complexity. Maeda also writes regularly on his Web log, his online diary. The name of the Web log, as you guessed, is *simplicity.*

Southwest Airlines know this.

Southwest is North America's most successful and profitable airline. It is also the most simple. There are no assigned seats, just groups. And the groups are based on the passenger's arrival time. Food is minimal.

There are also no hubs. The planes fly the shortest distance between two points. In other words, you won't be stopping in Atlanta or Chicago on every flight. All of this simplicity saves the passenger time and makes the company money.[3]

Papa John's knows this.

Papa John's makes great pizza. According to the founder, John Schnatter, the secret to the company's success has been its simplicity. Look at this statement found on their Web site:

At Papa John's we have a simple formula for success: Focus on one thing and try to do it better than anyone else. By keeping the Papa John's menu simple, we are able to focus on the quality of our product by using only superior-quality ingredients.[4]

People have embraced the simple menu and the simple philosophy. What began as one store just over twenty years ago has mushroomed into the third largest pizza franchise in the United States.

Interior designers know this.

Real Simple is the name of a popular interior design magazine and Web site (www.realsimple.com). People are responding to the concept. *Real Simple* has been the most successful magazine launch in a decade. The magazine promotes simple interior design and instructs readers how to keep their house, kitchen, and meals simple.

Even the king (or queen) of interior design, Martha Stewart, knows simple. Not because she lived the simple life in a prison cell but because she advocates simple design. *Perfect* and *simple* are two words commonly heard on her program and seen in her articles.

At least, that is what our wives tell us. We don't claim to know about Martha firsthand.

Marketing gurus know this.

Marketing and advertising executives are using simple slogans and advertising pieces. You know that because you have seen it. That is not all though. The revolution goes deeper than that. They are marketing their products as solutions for our complicated lives. The message is: "This product will simplify your life." They know people respond to simple.

In a notable marketing book, *Simplicity Marketing*, Steven Cristol and Peter Sealey teach executives to position their products to promise customers a more simple life.[5] They argue that an effective brand will reduce the stress of the customer. The value that many products offer is clutter reduction.

Take for example the marketing of the South Beach Diet. The diet market is cluttered. New diets and weight-loss strategies come along all the time, but South Beach promised the potential dieter something other plans failed to deliver: simplicity and less stress.

The founder and author of the South Beach Diet movement explains the essence of his diet this way: "What started as a part-time foray into the world of nutrition has led me to devise a simple, medically-sound diet that works, without stress, for a large percentage of those who try it."[6] Did you see it? Simple and stress-free. Besides a way for favorite desserts to actually be sugar-free, what more could dieters ask for?

OK. By now you get the point. Simple is in. Simple works. People respond to simple. But this book is directed to those passionate about effective church ministry. Does this simple revolution have any significance to churches and church leaders?

Keep reading.

Growing and vibrant churches know this.

In our extensive research of more than four hundred evangelical churches, we discovered the simple church revolution. We compared growing and vibrant churches to nongrowing and struggling churches. Church leaders from both groups completed the same survey, which was designed to measure how simple their church discipleship process was.

We anticipated that the vibrant churches would score higher. We anticipated that there would be a relationship between a simple process and church vitality, but the results were greater than we imagined. Our statistical consultant told us that we found something big.

There will be more discussion of the study in chapters to come, but here is the elevator conversation: The vibrant churches were much more simple than the comparison churches. The difference was so big that the probability of the results occurring with one church by chance is less than one in a thousand. Statistical people call this a relationship at the .001 level.

When a researcher finds a relationship at the .05 level, he calls his friends and brags. He knows he has found something worthwhile. When a researcher finds something at the .01 level, he calls his publicist and prepares to write. Finding something at the .001 level does not happen often. It's a big deal. If you're a stats person, it is "highly significant."

The significance is that, in general, simple churches are growing and vibrant. Churches with a simple process for reaching and maturing people are expanding the kingdom. Church leaders who have designed a simple biblical process to make disciples are effectively advancing the movement of the gospel. Simple churches are making a big impact.

Conversely, complex churches are struggling and anemic. Churches without a process or with a complicated process for making disciples are floundering. As a whole, cluttered and complex churches are not alive. Our research shows that these churches are not growing. Unfortunately, the overprogrammed and busy church is the norm. The simple church is the exception, yet our research shows that should not be the case.

The simple church revolution has begun.

Most churches are too busy to notice. They are on the outskirts of the movement, far removed from the revolution that is unfolding.

What We Are Not Saying

First, we are not suggesting that the simple approach to ministry is a change in doctrine or conviction. Thom has written several books on the primacy of sound, biblical, and orthodox doctrine in growing churches. On that issue we do not compromise.

Second, we are not saying that churches should become simple because it is in style or culturally hip. A revolution goes against the cultural grain. Churches that are simple are not mirroring the culture. They are not mimicking the world in order to reach the world.

In fact, the opposite is true. You must get this.

The culture is not simple. Not even close. Our world is not simple. Daily we experience information and decision overload. As the world is getting smaller and smaller (globalization through technology), things are getting more and more complex. In the midst of all the noise, all the rush, all the change, all the busyness, and all the uncertainty, people long for simplicity.

Precisely because things are so hectic and out of control people respond to simple. The busyness and complexity of life makes simple a great commodity, something desired. Simple churches intuitively know this. And because they are consumed with the call to make disciples, they have implemented a simple design for church ministry. They have designed a simple process to reach and mature people. Thus, these churches are getting people's attention and commitment.

Third, we also are not saying that churches should have a simple process just for pragmatic reasons (though it is working). More importantly, there is a theological and philosophical foundation on which a simple process stands. We will deal with this throughout the book, but here is a snapshot: While God never changes, He has chosen to work through a divine process.

For example, God chose to create the universe in a sequential and orderly process. He also designed His creation's maturation, including man, to occur in process. Spiritual growth (sanctification) is the process of a believer being transformed into the image of Christ. Simple churches have chosen to align themselves with the way God works. They have chosen to partner with the discipleship process revealed in Scripture. They have chosen to structure their churches around a simple process.

Fourth, we are also not claiming that a simple church design is easy. There is a big difference between simple and easy. Simple is basic, uncomplicated, and fundamental. Easy is effortless.

Ministry will never be easy. It is messy and difficult because people are messy and difficult. A simple process is not easy to implement or maintain. Leadership in the local church is extremely challenging. Leading a local church is neither easy nor simple, but the church strategy does not need to be complicated. The ministry design can and should be simple.

The Revolutionary

If anyone knows simple, it is Jesus.

If anyone is a revolutionary, it is Jesus. He is the original simple revolutionary. He stepped into a complicated and polluted religious scene. It was cluttered with Sadducees, Pharisees, Herodians, Zealots, and Essenes. He did not play by their rules. He could not stand their hypocrisy. He preferred spending time with tax collectors and sinners.

The religious leaders had developed a religious system with 613 laws. They chose the number 613 because that was how many separate letters were in the text containing the Ten Commandments. Then they found 613 commandments in the Pentateuch (the first five books of the Old Testament). They divided the list into affirmative commands (do this) and negative commands (don't do this).

There were 248 affirmative commands, one for every part of the human body, as they understood it. There were 365 negative commands, one for each day of the year. They further divided the list into binding commands and nonbinding commands. Then they spent their days debating whether the divisions were accurate and ranking the commands within each division.[7]

Enter Jesus. Jesus has the ability to take the complex and make it simple. A prime example is Matthew 22:37–40, where Jesus gives what has become known as the Great Commandment. Here is the scene. Jesus has just stumped the Sadducees. Literally. He silenced them by His wisdom (Matt. 22:34). Next up are the Pharisees. Maybe they can do a better job knocking this revolutionary down.

The Pharisees gather for a meeting. They devise a debate strategy. Their goal is to humiliate Jesus in front of the crowd. They choose their smartest guy, a lawyer, to take on Jesus. He asks Jesus which is the greatest commandment in the Law. Of all the 613 commandments, he is asking Jesus for the greatest. Jesus replied: "'Love the Lord your God with all your heart, with all your soul, and with all your mind.' This is the greatest and most important commandment. The second is like it: 'Love your neighbor as yourself.' All the Law and the Prophets depend on these two commandments."

Think about the significance of that moment. He said all the Law (and He added the Prophets) is summed up in this simple and perfect phrase. He was not lowering the standard of the Law. He was not abolishing it. He was capturing all its spirit, all of its essence, in one statement. He said all of it hangs on this. He summed up 613 commands in two. Jesus took the complexity and the advancement of the Law and made it very simple.

His Yoke

Jesus was a rabbi, a teacher. In the Jewish culture each rabbi had a yoke of teaching. His yoke was His instructions, His content, and His message. Many rabbis put yokes of teaching on the people that were impossible and legalistic. These yokes pushed people away from the grace of God instead of toward it.

These yokes burned people out and turned people off. Jesus stepped into the scene and said to a crowd one day:

> Come to Me, all you who are weary and burdened, and I will give you rest. Take My yoke upon you and learn from Me, because I am gentle and humble in heart, and you will find rest for your souls. For My yoke is easy and My burden is light.
> (Matt. 11:28–30)

Jesus said His yoke is easy. His teaching was in stark contrast to the religious rabbis of the day. He was not offering a complicated and long set of rules, rituals, and regulations. He was offering grace. He was offering a simple relationship with God.

Jesus and Clutter

As a simple revolutionary, Jesus was bothered by meaningless and distracting clutter. On at least one occasion, Jesus cleansed the temple. Many biblical scholars believe He did so twice during His earthly ministry.

Mark 11 gives the account of one of His cleaning projects. Jesus was enraged by what He observed in the temple. The temple had the appearance of being a place where people would seek God, but this was not the reality. People had lost their focus. Mark describes three areas of clutter that infuriated Jesus.

First, people were buying and selling in the temple. The people who came to worship God had to buy sacrifices. The leaders allowed vendors to set up shop in the temple. Historians reveal that vendors were typically set up outside the temple. Now the makeshift marketplace is inside the temple. Jesus responded by driving out those who were selling doves.

Second, money changers were exchanging currency for the Gentiles. The Gentiles needed Jewish money to buy sacrifices, and they were exploited with a fee for the exchange. Instead of the temple being a house of prayer for the Gentiles (all nations), it was cluttered with people robbing them financially. Jesus reacts by throwing over the tables of the money changers.

Third, the temple had become a shortcut for people to pass through the city. People were actually using the court of the Gentiles as a shortcut to carry things. Jesus stopped them.

His behavior in the temple gives us amazing insight into the heart of God. Jesus is adamantly opposed to anything that gets in the way of people encountering Him. He quoted from Isaiah that day saying, "Is it not written, 'My house will be called a house of prayer for all nations'? But you have made it 'a den of thieves'!" (Mark 11:17).

Many of our churches have become cluttered. So cluttered that people have a difficult time encountering the simple and powerful message of Christ. So cluttered that many people are busy *doing* church instead of *being* the church.

What about your church?

Fancy Coffins

In Matthew 23 Jesus confronted the leaders of spiritual hypocrisy and complexity. He told the Pharisees that they were like a fancy cup that is dirty. Everything looked good on the outside, but inwardly everything was disgusting. He also told them that they were like whitewashed tombs or top-of-the-line coffins. On the outside everything was shiny. Everything was presentable. But beneath the surface there was death. Beneath the surface there was emptiness.

Just like many churches.

The clutter can often make things look OK, even good. The busyness is a great disguise for the lack of life. The complexity is a great cover-up. Churches can sometimes be fancy coffins.

Several of the complex church leaders we talked with admitted their busy churches were void of life. Several knew their cluttered church calendars lacked direction. Several also admitted that all the activity was having little impact. Often great amounts of activity do not produce life change. It only gives the impression that things are happening, that there is life.

One complex church leader commented, "The project confirmed the reality that I was slow to face: we are not seeing spiritual transformation in the lives of our people. We have become content being busy."

Another e-mailed us and said, "Completing the survey has shown me how we desperately need to develop a simple process for spiritual transformation. Right now, we just have a lot of programs. I have already begun evaluating all that we presently do."

Perhaps we are losing ground not *despite* our overabundance of activity but *because* of it.

The Not-So-Simple Life II

Pastor Rush is now in his office. Before he returns the phone calls and e-mails, he decides to empty his bag. He pulls out his conference notebook along with some CDs and workbooks he purchased. He moves the materials to a place on his bookshelf.

The new materials are now sitting neatly next to other conference notebooks. He has seen plenty of church models and programs. Most of it is good stuff, and most of it has worked somewhere. Just not here. Not yet, anyhow. Not like he has dreamed, imagined, and prayed.

He recalls the advice of a speaker at a conference to take the best ideas from other churches and implement those ideas in your own church. He has tried to do that. He has pulled bits and pieces from different church models. He has implemented an array of programs. Pastor Rush's church is experiencing ministry schizophrenia.

Ministry schizophrenia is not a clinical disease. You will not find it in a psychology book, but it is present in many churches. You have noticed it before, but maybe you did not diagnose it as ministry schizophrenia. It is plaguing the local church. It occurs when churches and church leaders are not sure who they are. They are not clear what their fundamental identity is. They run in a disjointed and frantic fashion.

It occurs most often when churches attempt to blend multiple church models into one. They do so with good intentions. Like Pastor Rush, church leaders are often encouraged to pick and choose the best from a variety of church models. The problem is that the philosophy behind each model varies, sometimes in small ways and sometimes in big ways. Inevitably, the multiple ministry philosophies bump heads. And that is never pretty.

When ministry philosophies collide, schizophrenia happens. The church is unsure of who she is. Programs and ministries move in a multiplicity of directions. It seems as if there are multiple church personalities. No one really knows what to expect.

Ministry schizophrenia is not an environment conducive to spiritual transformation. People are pulled one way, then another. It is definitely not the picture Paul painted of the church, where the believers would be "standing firm in one spirit, with one mind, working side by side for the faith of the gospel" (Phil. 1:27).

Pastor Rush sits down in his chair, and looks at the bookshelf containing all the resources. He senses the church is not moving in a clear and coherent direction. He knows something must change. He feels pressure. The expectations from board members, staff, and others are great. However, his expectations and his burden are much greater.

Something must change, but Pastor Rush is struggling with where to begin. He understands the *what*. He has a sense of *what* the church should be doing. He believes the church should be committed to evangelism, prayer, helping people build relationships with believers, seeing people grow deeper, serving, and worship.

He also has a sense of the *why*. He deeply desires to see God glorified. He struggles with the *how*. One burning question has entered his mind: *How* can we structure all of this to come together to make disciples?

He is beginning to diagnose the problem. There is no overarching discipleship process that pulls everything together. There is not a clear process in place that streamlines the ministry and keeps everyone on the same page. There is no big picture. Pastor Rush has implemented programs and ministries without asking what they contribute to the whole.

Like many churches, success at Pastor Rush's church is measured by how well a particular program goes. Parts are evaluated but never the whole. He has never looked at each weekly program in light of a simple discipleship process. In fact, there is no process. There is no clear beginning and no clear end. There is only a bunch of programs.

Pastor Rush is having one of those "aha, I get it" moments. Maybe you are too. These moments are sacred but also scary. They are sacred because they lead to change. And they are scary because they lead to change.

Simultaneously, Pastor Rush feels both relief and frustration. Relief because he is seeing what the problem is. Frustration because he now knows the problem exists. He and his staff are just running programs. He committed to ministry to make disciples, and he has become a program manager.

He has not looked at the forest because he has been preoccupied with all the trees. Pastor Rush knows he must step back. He must take a look at his church with fresh eyes.

He must see the whole picture.

Seeing the Whole Picture

Jose Diaz saw the whole picture. One of the happiest days in his life was Sunday morning, August 7, 2005. It occurred at Christ Fellowship in Miami, Florida (the church where Eric serves as executive pastor). For the first time Jose was able to worship sitting next to his father, Luis Diaz. Luis had been a believer for many years, but had never attended church with his son, Jose.

He couldn't. He was in prison, for twenty-six years.

On Sunday, August 7, 2005, they worshipped together. Luis Diaz was released four days earlier because DNA testing had proven his innocence. He had been wrongfully convicted. Because of the evidence, he was no longer considered the Bird

Road rapist. You probably saw the story on the news. It made the national headlines.

The Bird Road rapist was on the prowl from 1977 to 1979. Many victims described him as an English-speaking Latin male, over six feet tall, and weighing approximately two hundred pounds. He sometimes took things from the victims.

After her attack, the first victim saw Luis Diaz at the gas station where she worked.

Four days earlier she provided police with a description: Latin male, six feet tall, about two hundred pounds, English-speaking, with a two-door green or black car. Luis Diaz drove into the gas station in his green four-door Chevrolet. The victim called the police with his license number, and she later identified him as her attacker from his driver license picture. Diaz weighed 134 pounds and was five feet three inches tall. He was married with three children. He spoke no English. At this time no charges were filed.

The attacks continued, and the public grew more and more concerned. The police focused on Diaz. Another victim made an identification of him from a photographic array. He was arrested in August 1979. Two days later fourteen victims viewed a live lineup. Five victims identified Diaz positively. Later several more victims identified Diaz from a video lineup. Prosecutors brought eight charges against him.

Luis Diaz insisted he was innocent and went to trial in May 1980. There was no physical evidence connecting Diaz to the crime. A search of Diaz's home produced no items taken from victims. No weapon was ever found. No semen or blood was found in Diaz's car, though four of the victims had been raped in the attacker's car. Most of the victims had described the attacker as taller and heavier.

Diaz, because of his job as a fry cook, reeked of onions after his night shift. None of the victims described an odor. Despite all the evidence to the contrary, Diaz was found guilty and sentenced to multiple life sentences.

In 1993, two victims came forward and recanted their identifications of Diaz. Jose, his son, began researching DNA testing and how it was used to overturn wrongful convictions. He knew his father was innocent. He wrote letters and partnered with groups such as the Innocence Project to produce a motion for DNA testing. DNA tests from two of the victims proved the same person raped them. It was not Diaz.

All charges were dropped, and Diaz was freed after twenty-six years.

Jose Diaz pushed to see the evidence from the testing. Jose Diaz insisted on seeing the whole picture. He saw the forest and not just the trees in the case of his father.

The few testimonies were only one slice of the picture, one tree in the forest. The whole picture involved the physical evidence, the DNA testing, the lack of weapon, and the police profile. The whole picture told a different story. Jose stepped back and looked with fresh eyes. And he got others to do the same. Because Jose was committed to the whole picture, he was a part of freeing his father.

Like Jose Diaz, church leaders are called to free prisoners. Not from physical jail cells but from spiritual ones. Leaders are called to offer freedom to those who are imprisoned by sin (see Luke 4:18).

Like Diaz, church leaders must see the whole picture. Leaders must see the forest and not just the trees. Being simple requires seeing the whole picture. Clutter often exists because church leaders see only part. More and more things are added without an understanding of how it all affects the whole.

To have a simple church, leaders must ensure that everything their church does fits together to produce life change. They must design a simple process that pulls everything together, a simple process that moves people toward spiritual maturity.

Designers

Simple church leaders are designers. They design opportunities for spiritual growth. Complex church leaders are programmers. They run ministry programs.

Church leaders who are programmers focus on one program at a time. Their goal, though never stated, is to make each program the best. Church leaders who are designers are focused on the end result, the overall picture. They are as concerned with what happens between the programs as with the programs themselves.

The simple church leaders we surveyed were expert designers. They were not the producers of spiritual growth and church vitality. Only God is the producer of the growth. But like the apostle Paul, these church leaders are expert builders (see 1 Cor. 3:10). They have skillfully designed an environment where life change is likely to occur. They have designed a simple process that moves people through stages of spiritual growth.

To have a simple church, you must design a simple discipleship process. This process must be clear. It must move people toward maturity. It must be integrated fully into your church, and you must get rid of the clutter around it.

It is much easier to write and read that paragraph than to make it happen. Church leaders struggle with implementing a process. In fact, church leaders admit that this is their biggest ministry struggle. They are the weakest in designing a comprehensive process for their churches.[8] It is no wonder that the majority of churches are stagnant or declining. It is hard to see the forest when leaders are constantly bumping into the trees.

Join us on a journey to explore the simple church revolution. Not only will you see the results of the major research study, but you will also learn to be a designer. You will learn to design a simple discipleship process.

Imagine a church where you, as a leader, can articulate clearly how someone moves from being a new Christian to become a mature follower of Christ. Imagine that your church is no longer just busy but is alive with ministries and activities that make a difference.

Such is the simple church revolution. Welcome to the journey.

At the end of each chapter we have included Group Discussion Questions. We encourage you to wrestle with the concepts presented in this book as a team. Use these questions with staff and/or volunteers that you serve alongside.

GROUP DISCUSSION QUESTIONS

1. In the culture how have you seen people respond to simple?
2. In what ways do you relate to Pastor Rush?
3. If you could give Pastor Rush some advice, what would it be?
4. Is our church simple or complex? Why?
5. Why is it so hard to see the big picture in ministry?
6. What do you think is required to design a process for church ministry?
7. Where do we fit on this continuum?

Programmer-------------------------------------Designer

The Simple
(and Not-So-Simple)
Church in Action

To be simple is to be great.
~ RALPH WALDO EMERSON

Both of us own houses in Florida. Florida is great, especially South Florida (Thom/Naples, Eric/Miami). The culture is rich. The food is amazing. The water is beautiful. The list goes on and on. The weather. Beaches. Palm trees. Sun. Fishing. Fresh fruit. Florida lobster. Great college football. Stone crab. Snorkeling. The weather.

Did we mention the weather?

The weather is the trump card. Click on weather.com during the winter and check out South Florida before you shovel snow, put on a flannel shirt, or take your cold medicine. Sorry to rub it in. Just speaking the truth in love.

The pictures do not fully capture the great weather. You cannot get the real feel from the travel channel or guidebooks at Barnes and Noble. Words and images fall short. You have to experience it. You have to observe it up close. The cool wind off the ocean. The breeze whistling through the palms. The refreshing air. The warm sun. The weather has to be tasted, smelled, sensed, and felt . . . in February.

The weather is the trump card.

Except during hurricane season. Floridians now speak Greek—not because they are active in a church where the pastor preaches from the original text. They know Greek because the Greek alphabet was used to name hurricanes. Recent hurricane seasons have been the worst ever.

An active hurricane season makes winters in the Midwest or Northeast desirable. Well, almost.

The news reports do not fully capture hurricane weather. The anxiety. The waiting. Watching the cone of error (or cone of death) on the news. Wondering if it is going to hit and where. Putting up shutters. Stocking up on water. Getting gas for the generator. Hurricanes are a pain even before they hit.

If a hurricane hits, life is altered. More than can be understood by watching CNN or FOX News. More than can be grasped by reading an article. More than can be sensed by browsing through some pictures online.

People who lived through Hurricane Andrew in Miami in 1992 still talk about it. It is a marker. There is life "before Andrew" and life "after Andrew." Andrew was a category five hurricane, the worst possible. Only three category five hurricanes have impacted the United States since hurricane measurements were implemented. Andrew was also the most expensive natural disaster in U.S. history before Hurricane Katrina hit New Orleans and the Gulf Coast.

The pictures and the news reports could not possibly capture what the people experienced. A night of terror. The howling of wind. Tornadoes. The sound of houses tearing apart. The rising of water. The morning after when nothing was recognizable. Weeks without power. Months without a roof. The loss of everything.

Words and pictures fall short.

To grasp fully the great or horrifying Florida weather, you have to experience it. It is the only way you can really "get it." Experience leads to understanding. Many things in life have to be observed in action to be fully understood. To understand completely you have to be there.

You just had to be there.

Have you ever used that phrase to describe something you experienced? Something you experienced but could not quite describe. The moment was so powerful. It was clear and vivid. It resonated deeply within you. Yet you were having a hard time articulating it. So you gave up trying to explain it. You summed it up with, "You just had to be there."

Such is the case with the simple church.

You just have to be there. You have to see it. In action.

Seeing Simple

We have seen it. We have observed the simple church in action. We want you to see it too. We want you to be there. The research and the implications will make more sense to you if you could see it. The data will resonate more with you if you could just be there. So you are invited.

We are inviting you to join us on a church consultation trip. You will see a simple church in action. And you will see a not-so-simple one.

Some church consulting can be accomplished through phone conversations and electronic communication. Recommendations on issues like parking, staff planning, program implementation, and community analysis do not necessarily require an on-site visit. For example, there should be enough parking to handle full capacity in the auditorium and the education space (including children and youth). On average, 1.8 persons use one parking spot. The church should make plans to provide parking options based on this estimate, so that parking does not become a lid that prevents growth. A consultation like this can occur over the phone.

This type of church consulting, however, has its limits. Reports and pictures fall short. The culture of a church does not come out on paper or over the phone. Church culture is sensed. It is perceived. It is felt, sniffed, tasted, and observed in action. It can only be accomplished through a site visit.

A site visit is a multiple-day trip to the site of a local church. The church is analyzed on paper before the trip so that the time there may be maximized. Staff meetings, worship services, and people interaction are all observed. Personal interviews are conducted with staff and volunteers. Analysis is conducted on the health, culture, and the potential of the church.

In this chapter you will join us for an extensive on-site consultation with two churches. One of the churches is a simple church. The other is not. They are of similar size and are in similar communities. Both of these churches are real, but their names have been changed.

You will see what we see and hear what we hear. Look beneath the surface. Observe things with a fresh set of eyes. Write down your observations in the margins. Think critically. Analyze and evaluate. Be there.

First Church

Our first visit is to First Church. First Church has been in existence for over forty years. They are recognized throughout their denomination for being a solid church with great programs. In fact, other churches have emulated their community Christmas program. They are also known for having talented and popular staff members. They have the type of staff members who speak at events, pray on the platform at conventions, and write articles.

The church has been at a standstill for five years. The church has not grown, and minimal numbers of people have come to know Christ. While things are not great, they are OK. The church has experienced some staff turnover but no major turmoil. There has been some unrest in the congregation but no major rift. In other words, they have not hit a point of crisis.

And without a point of crisis, it is difficult to change.

Cross Church

Our second visit is to Cross Church. Cross Church is not that well-known. We had not even heard about the church until the consultation. It is in a less-known part of the country than First Church. We recognized none of the staff members' names.

The church has been in existence for just under twenty years. Over the last several years, the church has grown a lot. The initial analysis was exciting. People have come to know Christ, and they have stayed at the church. They have gotten plugged into ministry and are contributing to the body of Christ.

First Church Statements

On the drive to First Church, we review several documents the church has sent us. Most churches have these types of documents: church bulletins, newsletters, staff manuals, annual budgets, brochures, and ministry booklets. We read them, seeking to discern the focus of the church, the top priorities, and the ministry approach.

Most churches have a lot of information to communicate, but First Church also has a lot of statements. There is a mission statement, a purpose statement, a vision statement, and a strategy statement. Each statement is different from the other. And long.

Looking more at the brochures, we notice that each ministry department also has different statements. Each statement is intended to describe the focus or direction of the church. There are more than ten different statements on the materials we are reviewing.

What does it mean?

The mission statement listed in the bulletin is "to lead unsaved people to become fully devoted followers of Christ." Obviously, someone has been influenced by the ministry of Willow Creek. The purpose statement printed on the church brochure features five "M" words: *Magnification, Multiplication, Maturity, Ministry,* and *Mission*. Some leader had been impacted by Rick Warren and the purpose-driven movement. The vision statement highlighted on the church stationary is "loving this community to Christ." Or maybe that is the strategic statement.

Nevertheless, it was *another* statement.

It would be easier to memorize the book of James than to memorize all the statements . . . and much more profitable.

Do the statements have anything to do with one another? Are they reflected in how the church actually does ministry?

Or are they just placed on top of an existing paradigm and structure? The confusion with the multiple statements indicates that there may be a multiplicity of ministry philosophies and approaches existing in the same place. It is especially unclear how all these statements fit together.

We are unsure of the real focus of the church. These documents do not make it clear. Perhaps the upcoming interviews with staff and key lay leaders will enlighten us. We pull into the parking lot. You are grateful to be here . . . alive. You think to yourself, *Thom is a really bad driver.*

Interviewing the First Church Pastor

We meet briefly with the pastor of First Church. He is gracious and excited about the time we will have together. You can tell he wrestles back and forth between giving the perception that everything is OK and admitting that he is frustrated. He has grown increasingly bothered and tired with the activity in his church. Not because he is lazy but because it is not producing the spiritual fruit he longs to see.

He also hints that he feels the church is disjointed and headed in multiple directions. He is excited about the great things that are happening in different ministries in the church and does not want to pour cold water on the energetic staff who lead them. At the same time he senses that not everyone is on the same page.

We ask him *what* his desire for the church is. *What* does he believe God is calling First Church to do? He speaks of a church where lives are changed. Good. We ask him *how* his church is set up to make that happen. He struggles to answer. He indicates this is the reason he has asked us to come.

Interviewing First Church Leaders

During interviews with key lay leaders, we ask what the focus of their church is. We get a myriad of responses:

"Providing great worship services and big events for people."

"Excelling in our ministry to children."

"Taking care of the needs in our church family."

"Addressing social and political injustices in our community."

"Having small groups that are relationally structured."

"Having small groups that teach the Bible."

Of all the vision/mission statements we read in the car, not one is mentioned by the staff and other church leaders. Not even close. The people in the church have not internalized those statements. They are really hazy on what the church direction is. We ask the staff to quote their vision or purpose. Few are able to do so. Despite all the fancy brochures with well-crafted statements, there is not a clear *what* at First Church. The church is not united around a singular purpose.

If the *what* of First Church is unclear, the *how* is not even on the radar. If the purpose is hazy, the process for making the purpose happen has not entered the picture. When we ask the staff and key lay leaders what the church's process for discipleship is, we get blank stares. Confused looks. We rephrase the question. Several times. How do you structure your church to make disciples? How do set up your ministry programs to move people toward spiritual transformation? More blank stares. Some stuttering.

The best response: "Basically, it just sort of happens."

Unfortunately at First Church, what is supposed to *just sort of happen* isn't.

Cross Church Statement

On the drive to Cross Church, we review the same type of documents. The number and types of brochures, newsletters, bulletins, and other documents are about the same. The quality of the brochures and bulletins is similar. The graphic design is comparable.

One major difference emerges. There is only one statement—just one.

While First Church has a lot of statements, Cross Church has one. There is one overarching theme. One statement. It is short. Though it is adapted for each age group, the thrust is the same. It is clear that Cross Church is all about "loving God, loving people, and serving the world." Simple.

Their focus is to lead people to love God, love others, and serve the world. It is clear and concise, and it is reinforced on all their communication pieces. But we wonder if this is really in the DNA of the church. We wonder if this statement is embedded in the culture of Cross Church. Is it reflective of reality? Is it directive of the ministry? We pull into the parking lot eager to interview staff and key leaders to find out what is behind this one statement.

Interviewing the Cross Church Pastor

When we meet the pastor at Cross Church, we tell him we noticed right away that there is a lot of consistency with the "love God, love others, serve the world" theme. He indicates that this is what the church is all about.

You are feeling bold since this is your second consultation. So you jump in and engage in a dialogue with the pastor.

"So, that is your purpose, right?"

"I guess you could say that."

"Talk to us about your process. How do you make your purpose happen?"

"Love God, love others, serve the world is our process."

"I thought you said it was your purpose."

"It is both. Our purpose is a process."

"Oh."

Interesting. Genius. Simple. Instead of a chasm of separation between their purpose and their process, the two are one in the same. Instead of distancing the *what* and the *how*, Cross Church has combined them. The purpose and the process are married at Cross Church. The two have become one. Their purpose (loving God, loving people, and serving the world) is a process.

We ask him to explain what led to this. Here is what happened.

Several years ago the pastor knew that something was missing. Each year many people visited the church, joined the church, or became Christians. Yet the church was not growing. As many people were leaving as were coming. The back door was as big as the front door.

More importantly, people were not being transformed. The church was not healthy. New programs and special events were constantly implemented to remedy the problem, but the busier the church became, the more the problem was amplified.

Problems are always bigger when everyone is tired.

He began to ask some hard questions. He decided to step back and see the big picture, to see the forest and not just the trees. He became convinced that what was missing was a simple process that moved people toward spiritual maturity.

He knew both biblically and experientially that spiritual transformation is a process. He desired to design a simple process that would facilitate the process of spiritual transformation in people. He committed to developing a process for making disciples, a process that pulled everything together and executed the purposes of the church.

He invested months praying through his dream for the church. He was expecting something new and profound to emerge. Nothing new or profound came. There was not a big, holy, goose-bump moment. He went back to praying and reading. He settled on an old dream, an old vision: Make disciples.

Just so you know, he stole that from Jesus. A plagiarized biblical vision is always a good thing.

The pastor's dream was not original or unique. It was simply to "make disciples" (Matt. 28:19), disciples who would be mature in Christ (Eph. 4:13). This revelation led to deeper thinking and more questions. What does a mature disciple look like? He spent a lot of time in Scripture wrestling with this question.

He believed God wanted disciples who would walk intimately with Christ, live in community with others, and serve both the church and the world. Those several aspects of discipleship fascinated him. He also believed that this was a process, that people did not become this kind of disciple overnight. He began to meet with others about structuring Cross Church to help people become this kind of disciple.

The group met and prayed. They wanted a vision that the church could really grab hold of. To eliminate confusion, they decided that there would be one rallying cry that would feature the discipleship process. "Love God, love others, and serve the world" best captured it.

The pastor explains that the statement emphasizes that discipleship is a process. First, someone loves God. This first step is the most basic and essential aspect of discipleship, but it does not end there. After someone enters into a love relationship with God, he or she begins to love others. The person commits to grow in community with others. After loving God and others, the natural result is to serve people. And the process continues. It is ongoing.

Interviewing Cross Church Leaders

After the meeting with the pastor, we interview some staff and key leaders. The vast majority of the people to whom we speak talk freely about loving God, loving others, and serving the world. The people at Cross Church have grasped the process. We discover that it is discussed regularly in staff meetings, lay leadership meetings, and is referred to frequently in worship services. There is a diagram of the process in the office, and every staff member can say it with ease. It is in the DNA of the church.

Cross Church is committed to loving God, loving others, and serving others. It is great that it is on paper and in the minds of the people. But how do they make this ideal happen? How is this vision translated to regular church life? We began to ask leaders these questions.

One church member responds by saying, "The worship service helps me love God more, and my small group is where I learn to really love others. I am also a greeter which I know is a small thing, but I feel like I am serving others in that way."

One church leader says, "We ask people to do three things a week here. Come to a worship service to fall more in love with God and His Word. Go to a small group to love others in community. Serve in a ministry to impact others. Love God, love others, serve the world. We really try to keep it that simple."

A longtime staff member comments, "We believe our process and programs have to be in partnership. We discussed what the best programs were for each level of the process, and we committed to doing only those things." In other words, they decided to set up the weekly programs sequentially. Therefore, people could move through the process simply by moving from one program to the next.

Programming at First Church

We learn a lot by walking around First Church for several days. Watching the preparation for the programs. Talking to people who are passionate about what they are leading or attending. We observe a lot because there is a lot to observe.

Each week First Church has a Sunday morning worship service, a Sunday night worship service, Sunday morning Sunday school, Wednesday night discipleship classes, home groups, Tuesday morning men and women's meetings, and Thursday night visitation.

In case you lost count, that is eight major programs. Eight programs in seven days. This lineup is just for adults. It does not count what all the different age groups offer, things like youth choir and children's choir. This is each week. Every week. The normal stuff. The stuff normal people are supposed to do.

We wonder how First Church members can know their neighbors, the unchurched next door.

We sit in on some of the programs. They are good. People seem to enjoy them. It is hard to say which ones should be eliminated. However, it is clear that attention is divided. It is hard to be excellent when you are focused on so much. This reality shows up in the small things. Everyone is short on leaders. Sound guys are pulled all over the place. Some rooms are not cleaned. Some people complain their ministry is not publicized enough.

While walking around, we ask staff and leaders some basic questions. "What is the program that you expect the majority of your guests to attend?" Or, "What program do you teach your people to invite their friends and neighbors to?" We get unclear answers. Some leaders say every program. Others debate over which program it is.

There is no process, so it does not surprise us that there is not a beginning point. There is also no connection between all the statements we read and the programs that are offered.

When we ask what program they attempt to move new members or guests to, we get more confused looks. Some people get defensive. People are accustomed to defending and justifying the existence of their particular program. The programs are ends in themselves. They are not used as tools to move people toward spiritual maturity.

We also learn about all the special events. There are a lot of them, but the main one is the Christmas program. It is huge. It is a big budgeted item, and people spend months preparing for it. They begin in August, and it involves everyone. And lots of animals too. Not stuffed ones either. They are really proud of the live animals. But some of the staff members are bitter about the Christmas program because they say it burns everyone out until March.

We ask some members how effective the Christmas program is. We could tell that is an odd question to them. We are assuming the goal is to reach people in the community, so we ask how many guests come. And how many of the people who come don't go to church. We find out that the attendees are mostly people from other churches. "But it is such a great tradition."

There is a story in the Gospel of Mark about traditions and about a program being the focus. Jesus was picking some grain, and the religious people fussed at Him. He was hungry, but they were upset because He was "working" on the Sabbath. The Sabbath had been given for man to rest, but these religious leaders changed the focus. In their minds, the Sabbath as a program had to be protected. The focus became the day itself and not the result that was intended for the people.

Jesus said, "The Sabbath was made for man, and not man for the Sabbath" (Mark 2:27).

Programs were made for man, not man for programs. If the goal is to keep certain things going, the church is in trouble. The end result must always be about people. Programs should only be tools.

Programming at Cross Church

We learn a lot by walking around Cross Church for several days.

The simple process is experienced weekly through the programs the church offers. The weekly programs are tools to help people love God, love others, and serve the world. If the programs were not used to move people through the process, then the vision/process statement would be meaningless.

The first step in the process is to *love God*, and the weekend worship services are used to help people do so. The worship service is where guests, new people, and nonbelievers enter the church. It is also the weekly event where believers draw close to God through inspiring worship and dynamic biblical teaching.

The second step in the process is to *love others*, so the next program in the process is designed to help people connect relationally. The weekend services do not connect people to others very well. Like most churches, people sit facing forward and have little interaction with one another.

The staff concluded that small groups were the best environment for people to love one another in biblical community. Some small groups are on campus on Sundays or Wednesdays. Some groups meet off campus in homes or restaurants. People are encouraged to plug into one group.

The third step in the process is to *serve the world*, and ministry teams engage people in ministry. People enjoy camaraderie in a team environment while experiencing the joy of serving others. Some of the teams focus on the church while others focus on the community. New members are told at the new member's class that they should not join the church if they do not plan on serving.

At Cross Church, there are three main programs. One for each phase in their process. They are placed strategically and sequentially along their process. The goal is to move people from program to program so people naturally progress through the process of spiritual transformation. People who attend worship services are encouraged to move to a small group. People in small groups are challenged to serve on a team.

It seems to be all they do. Three weekly programs. It is a simple design.

Staff Meetings

During the site visit to both churches, we are invited to attend the staff meetings. On both occasions we sit in chairs pushed back from the table. We are just here to observe.

Both First Church and Cross Church have their ministry staff meetings on Tuesday. Both meetings begin with a devotional thought and a time of prayer. Both meetings are about the same length of time. Both meetings have an agenda. Both meetings are in the church conference room. From a distance the meetings are similar.

Up close the meetings are very different.

A lot can be learned by sitting in these meetings and comparing them. We observe some stark differences in some common facets of church staff meetings.

The Calendar at First Church

If you serve on a staff, you are familiar with "the calendar." It is a part of every staff meeting. First Church and Cross Church both have calendars. We all do. Even Floridians. They will always exist. Reviewing them in staff meeting is necessary no matter how boring the time is.

First Church spends a lot of time in the meeting dealing with the calendar. This activity, however, does not seem to be wasted time. It is a necessity because so much is on the calendar. Management of all the activities requires skillful coordination and oversight. The facility space has to be juggled, the communication pieces have to be crafted, and the cleaning of the campus has to be scheduled differently each week.

The staff jockey for a position on the calendar, wanting a particular event to be the only event for a specific day. They use the typical calendar request form system, and the staff member who submits the form first declares that day sacred for his or her event. A lot of time is spent coordinating specific ministry calendars with the overall church calendar.

The Calendar at Cross Church

The calendar viewing time is different at Cross Church. Cross Church's staff spends less than five minutes looking at the calendar. After first observing the staff meeting at First Church, this contrast seems absurd.

Are they poor managers? Are they just ignoring all the details that need to be handled? Why does it take so much less time to deal with the calendar?

It is not that they are unable to coordinate; it is simply that the calendars are pretty empty. A staff social is the only non-weekly event on the calendar in the next month. The time First Church staff spent on calendaring, Cross Church staff devotes to discussing the weekly ministry programs. During this particular meeting, the staff evaluates how the weekend worship services are working as part of the discipleship process.

Numbers at First Church

During staff meeting both churches look at the numbers of people attending. That is surprising because typically non-growing churches rarely do. First Church has not grown in several years. Each staff member at both churches gets a weekly report that shows how many people attended various programs. However, the analysis of this report is different. You must not miss the distinction.

First Church looks at the numbers of people involved in each program. Each program is viewed separately from the whole. Each staff member checks the number of people in his favorite program and declares things are great. For the youth ministry, it is the Wednesday night event. For the worship pastor, it is the number of people in his choir. For the children's ministry, it is the number of children at the Sunday morning program.

Numbers at Cross Church

Cross Church looks at the numbers of people at different stages in their ministry process. They evaluate how many people are at the *love God* stage (worship service), the *love others* stage (small groups), and the *serve the world* stage (ministry teams). They look at a quarterly report that shows the increase or decrease in these programs as it relates to their process.

During this staff meeting they are concerned that the *love God* stage (worship service attendance) has increased 10 percent over the last quarter but that the *serve the world* stage (ministry teams) has not increased proportionally. Their simple process is designed to move people from worship services to small groups to places of service, so this report alarms them. They discuss ways to encourage new people to begin serving.

Did you see the distinction?

Here it is. Read this carefully. First Church staff members view the numbers *vertically* while Cross Church views them *horizontally*.

First Church analyzes the numbers of each program apart from all the other programs. They look at each program in isolation from all the other ones. Analysis is on the programs, not an overarching process. Each staff member or ministry leader has tunnel vision about his or her program. They look up and down, not side to side.

Cross Church staff members see things differently, from side to side.

Cross Church has set up their programs to move people through their process. They monitor this movement through their attendance patterns. When they look at reports, they focus on assimilation. They are looking for movement. Movement is horizontal. Cross Church looks at the numbers to analyze the movement of people through the process.

New Ideas

New ideas and new opportunities often surface in staff meetings.

Where there are passionate leaders and passionate volunteers, there is always an abundance of new ideas. Combine this passion with the many needs that are prevalent in the lives of church members, and you have the equation for new programs and special events.

You have seen it. Everyone knows there is a need. And it is a legitimate need, not just a perceived one. Maybe it is that people are not being financial stewards, or marriages are falling apart. God lays it on someone's heart to do something. So far so good. What happens next is what separates a simple church from a complex one.

During the consultation with First Church and Cross Church, we observe both firsthand. Both staff teams are concerned about the marriages and the families in their church. During both staff meetings new opportunities for equipping families are discussed. They both offer a solution. One is complex. One is simple.

Observe the difference.

First Church and New Ideas

First Church is hosting two special events this month. One is an all-day Saturday marriage conference. The other is a two-day parenting seminar. The children's ministry is hosting the parenting seminar. The adult ministry is hosting the marriage conference.

No one wants to admit the two events are competing for the time of many of the same people. Ironically, some do not even see this is a problem. They don't see the two conflicting with each other because the events are on different weekends. They think that families should be willing to give two entire weekends to church programs in the same month. And they should be plugged into all regular weekly programs as well. So much for family time.

The promotion of both events is occupying a lot of time. Secretaries are spending half of their time making phone calls, working with vendors, and mailing out publicity pieces. Ministers are spending time organizing the event and begging people to come.

Registration is low. Frustration is high. Appropriate time is not being invested in the weekly programs. Most people don't see how much time is spent. They only see the final product.

Cross Church and New Ideas

Cross Church has the same needs. The staff is deeply burdened for the families at the church. Just like the staff at First Church. Marriages are falling apart. Parents need instruction on how to raise their children.

Cross Church responds differently. While they are using similar curriculum to First Church, they offer it in different venues. There are no special events on the calendar. Instead, they choose to meet the needs through their ministry process. They choose to offer the content through their existing programs.

Cross Church has started several small groups that will deal with these issues. Not only is the content presented, but the participants engage in a small group. They get relationally connected to people experiencing the same type of struggles.

Cross Church seeks to move people from their worship services to small groups, and these special groups are helping make that happen. People are getting both the content and the small group experience at the same time. More people respond because they are not away from home an entire weekend.

Registration is high. Frustration is low. The staff is using their time to organize and promote programs that are within the process. The people are not bombarded with too many options. There is no inward competition. Cross Church is able to move people through the discipleship process and meet these specific needs simultaneously. It is a win-win.

Staffing Decisions

Spending time with staff during a consultation always leads to key insight, especially hallway conversations. One of the most common hallway questions church leaders ask is, "Where can I find a minister to lead this ministry?" Both First Church and Cross Church are looking for staff. During the conversations about possible people to fill a vacancy, some key insights emerge.

Staffing at First Church

First Church is looking for the best staff possible. Makes sense, right? This reality is clearly stated by the leaders involved in the search for new staff. The goal is to assemble an all-star type staff, the best available in each role. The assumption is that this will make the greatest impact on the church and the community. The assumption has the appearance of wisdom but is faulty.

It has proven faulty for First Church. Their present staff is full of gifted people, but they are running in different directions. The stated philosophy is "hire thoroughbreds and let them run." Sounds good. But the more we talk to the staff, the more we realize there were multiple ministry philosophies on staff. Hiring the best did not pull the team together. Each person came aggressive and passionate for his or her own ministry without a commitment to the whole. People were not recruited and hired to join a coherent and unified movement.

The problem is not a lack of interviewing or reference checking. The problem is not a lack of passion. First Church does extensive interviewing, and the staff apparently walks with God. The problem is that there is no overarching process to recruit and rally staff. Recruiting talented staff with different ministry philosophies or approaches is a foundation for frustration and disaster.

Here is a snapshot of the First Church staff (the names have been changed). Pastor John is the pastor responsible for the student ministry. Pastor Bill is responsible for the adult education including Sunday school/small groups. Both are passionate about evangelism. It is what they both have focused on throughout their ministries. They have been known for building evangelistic ministries. It is what attracted the pastor and search team to both of these staff members. Sounds like they would get along. Seems like they would be a great team.

Not exactly.

The two agree theologically. Their eyes widen when talking about evangelism and the call to make disciples. Both believe lost people must hear the gospel. However, they are not on the same page philosophically. They approach evangelism differently. Pastor Bill believes in formal evangelism training. He has built his ministry on this approach. Pastor John believes in servant evangelism, and he has built his ministry on this approach. On paper the two coexist. In reality, the two philosophies bump heads.

On Thursday night, Pastor Bill offers formal evangelism training. He invites the entire church. He is always promoting it. He gets the senior pastor to mention it from the pulpit. He also does not understand why Pastor John does not encourage the students to be there. On Saturday mornings Pastor John offers servant evangelism opportunities. Adults and teenagers serve people in tangible ways.

Bill's supporters believe John's approach is shallow. John's supporters believe Bill's approach is cold. Some parents who attend Bill's group do not want their teenagers to attend John's group. The two groups are in a constant unspoken competition. Bill and John are theologically aligned but not philosophically. They were the best available in their fields, but they both struggle with being on staff, partly because of the other one.

They smile in the hallway and hug each other's families, but there is a big distance. Neither one is wrong. Neither one is less godly. They are just different at the core. And the pastor does not want to play referee.

Staffing at Cross Church

Cross Church is also looking for staff, but their questions are different. What they are seeking is different. Like First Church, they want people who are blameless in character and competent in their ministry calling. However, they are also looking for people who are on board with their ministry process. This is important to them.

Each existing staff member was recruited on the *love God, love others, serve the world* process. Some talented and highly recommended staff members were not considered because they had their own pet programs. And these programs fell outside of this ministry process. So the potential staff person was not considered.

Cross Church is more concerned with having a united staff than an all-star one.

If they are seeking a student minister, they are seeking one who will lead students to love God, love others, and serve the world. If they are seeking an adult pastor, they are seeking one who will lead adults to love God, love others, and serve the world. They are rigorous about this during the interviewing. They are that passionate about their process. And that consistent.

The staff members to whom we speak do not feel restrained. They feel free. They feel free because they are also passionate about the process. It is not just something they signed off on but something they longed to be a part of. They are thrilled to be involved in a church that views ministry the same way they do. Some helped create the process. Others committed to it before coming on staff.

The bounds are clear, and they are encouraged to implement and execute the ministry process with creativity and freedom. The existing staff members are not carbon copies of one another. They don't dress alike or talk alike. They don't like the same types of music or read the same type of books, but they are on the same page about how ministry happens at Cross Church.

The Announcements

It may seem strange to end this chapter with the announcements. However, most worship services end with some version of announcements.

We have learned that the announcements given during the worship services can tell a lot about the church. They typically are a good indication of the priorities of the church. During the announcements, people hear what is going on in the life of the church. People are asked to participate in something else.

Both First Church and Cross Church give announcements. Both use a pastor to do so. Both give them at similar times in the service. The content of the announcements is where the difference lies.

First Church Announcements

First Church gives a lot of announcements. People are invited to everything. The Sunday we are here, they announce eight different things. All with passion. All with the "this will change your life and you must come" tone. It is an infomercial, without the 800 number.

As the announcements roll on for several minutes, we look around. We wonder how these people are going to decide which program to go to next. We wonder what is in their minds.

It is an appropriate summation of our visit to First Church.

There is a lot of activity. A lot of busyness. And a lot of complexity. All of it can be justified by the right spokesperson. It just does not fit into a big picture. There is no big picture, no process that guides the ministry.

Cross Church Announcements

The announcements at Cross Church last about four minutes. There are three announcements. Here they are:

There is a guest reception for first-time guests. There is a new members' class next week for people who are interested in joining the church. And for those ready to try a small group, there is a small group information booth in the hallway.

Each announcement is about movement to the next step. People in the audience know exactly what they are invited to next. They are not bombarded with too much information. Three announcements. Simple. But what else would we expect?

It is an appropriate summation of our visit to Cross Church.

There is a lot of focus. A lot of clarity. Everything fits into the big picture. Everything is guided by their simple process for making disciples.

The Simple Church Experience

We leave First Church impressed with the staff and the members. Their commitment to Christ is real. But so many of the people at First Church are tired and confused on how to "do church."

Likewise, we leave Cross Church impressed with the people and the members. But we did not see weariness and frustration on the faces of the people at Cross Church. Instead we saw excitement, joy, and anticipation.

Two real churches. Two very different experiences.

Is your church more like First Church or Cross Church?

Would you like your church to be more like Cross Church?

Is it possible for your church to make such a radical change?

To those questions we now turn.

GROUP DISCUSSION QUESTIONS

1. How are we like First Church?
2. How are we like Cross Church?
3. Which church would you rather serve? Attend?
4. What advice would you give the pastor at First Church?
5. Describe the concept of process. Why is it important?
6. How can a ministry process help us eliminate some things?
7. How can a ministry process unite a staff?

THREE

Simple Church: An Extreme Makeover

*The ability to simplify means to eliminate the unnecessary
so that the necessary may speak.*
~ HANS HOFMANN

Clarity ➤➤ Movement ➤➤ Alignment ➤➤ Focus

xtreme Makeover: Home Edition is a successful television show. It is often inspiring, funny, and heartwarming. By the end of each episode, there is a huge lump in your throat.

The lump in your throat usually forms when the bus drives away and the family sees their new home for the first time. The lump grows as you watch the family walk into their newly renovated house. The lump is about to explode out of your throat when the last room is unveiled to one of the family members.

The last room is typically the "special room" that Ty, the team leader, designed. It is an act of grace. Watching the reaction of the recipient of this grace is stirring. Grace always is.

The church can learn a lot from this show.

According to 1 Peter 4:10, we are to be managers of God's grace. He has entrusted us with His grace. Trusted us with it. We are to be managers, stewards, and dispensers of His grace. The church must pour out God's grace to the world so that people may grow in His grace.

Like the homes on the television show, many churches need an extreme makeover. And the intended result of such a makeover must be the intersection of people with God's grace. For people to best experience and grow in God's grace, many churches need a redesign.

On *Extreme Makeover: Home Edition* families are selected to have their homes redone, fixed up, redesigned, or made over. The families are typically in desperate need of such a service. Ty and the design team show up at the family's home and announce they have been selected. The family is then ushered away for a week of vacation, usually somewhere in Florida.

While they are gone, the miracle of a new home takes place. The design team and others work almost around the clock to make it happen. It takes one week. If you have ever been involved in a church building project, you envy the amount of work done in one week. We assume the design team has some connections with the local governments and the code enforcers.

Sometimes a home requires a lot of tweaking. Some walls are knocked out. An additional room is added. The décor, furniture, landscaping, and color scheme are updated.

Other times, the house is completely rebuilt. The old blueprints are tossed. The new house is designed from a blank sheet of paper. The existing house is torn down, and a new one is constructed—from scratch.

The same is true for churches.

Some churches need some tweaking, while others need to

redesign completely. Regardless, our research shows that *extreme makeover: church edition* is necessary for many churches.

We don't mean the décor and color scheme.

We don't mean the floor plan of the auditorium or the footprint of the children's ministry space.

We are not talking about the building.

We mean the design for discipleship. We mean the design of church ministry. We are talking about how a church is designed and structured so people can be transformed by God's grace.

Designing

Just as Ty and his team are designers, so are church leaders.

Church leaders must craft opportunities where people will encounter the grace of God. Simple church leaders are designers, not programmers. They excel in designing a ministry process that leads to spiritual growth and vitality.

Spiritual growth is a process. It always has been. Thus, it would make sense for church leaders to design their churches around the process of spiritual growth.

In 1 Corinthians 3, believers are called God's children (v. 1), God's field (v. 9), and God's building (v. 9).

We are God's children. We begin as spiritual babies because we are born again (John 3:3). Our movement into spiritual adulthood is a process. That process is critical. Just as babies need the right environments to grow physically, people need the right environment to grow spiritually.

We are God's field. Fields do not bear fruit or crops on command. They blossom in process, and to do so properly, they need the right environment and the right nutrients.

We are God's building, God's spiritual house. He first built us (created us). He then bought us back (redeemed us) with His own blood. Next, He moved in. He took up residence in our lives. And He is not done. He continually works on us. He is constantly redecorating. Continual transformation is the work of the Holy Spirit.

Our wives and the Holy Spirit have a lot in common. It is not enough for our wives to move into a home. That is only the beginning. Redecorating is a must. And this is not a one-time redecorating. It keeps going and going.

The same is true with the Holy Spirit. Continual work is inevitable. It is never done. It is a lifelong process.

Children, fields, and buildings grow in process. They do not mature overnight. They are not built in a day. They are constantly redecorated.

Children, fields, and buildings need the right environments to facilitate the process of growth. Children need nurturing, touch, food, and love. Fields need water, care, and farming. Buildings need workers, materials, and someone like Ty.

Simple church leaders get this.

Not only do simple church leaders understand that spiritual transformation is a process, but they also respond to this reality. They do so by implementing a ministry process to facilitate this spiritual growth in people. They design a simple process and abandon everything else. They rely on their simple process to create the environments conducive to spiritual growth.

Defining a Simple Church

Here it is. Here is the definition for a simple church:

A simple church is *a congregation designed around a straight-forward and strategic process that moves people through the stages of spiritual growth.*

This definition has some weight to it.

Let's walk through the definition one phrase at a time.

The church is *designed*. It is not carelessly thrown together. It is not haphazardly planned. The ministry does more than "just happen." It is thought-out. It is structured. It is designed with care.

Also, it is designed *around* . . .

The design of the church is centered on something. The programs and ministries revolve around something. They are just not plugged into the church calendar and brochure. Everything is designed around something. And that something is not a nebulous abstract concept. The design for discipleship in a simple church revolves around the process.

A simple church is designed around *a straightforward and strategic process*.

The process is *straightforward*. It is not confusing; it is easy to grasp. The leaders know it, and the people understand it. The process is intentionally kept simple. It is not lengthened. It does not change every few months.

The church sticks to the simple process. Complexity is not welcome. More programs are not added to the process. The church rejects the multitude of new programs and models offered to it.

Since the process is the *how*, it is also *strategic*. The process is tied to the purpose or vision of the church. The two are closely knitted. The process is built for execution, to impact people. It is designed to be sequential so that people may move through the process.

The process *moves people* . . .

The simple and strategic process promotes movement. The process flows logically. People are attracted to Christ and the church and then are moved to points of attachment. The programs are used as tools to promote this movement.

And the movement through the straightforward and strategic process has an intentional and intended end result . . .

The process moves people *through the stages of spiritual growth*.

The goal is to partner with God to move people through the stages of spiritual growth. Changed lives are the bottom line, the intended end result. Christ formed in people is the goal.

A simple church understands that people are at different places in their spiritual journey, that spiritual growth is a process. The church is designed to partner with God to move people through stages of spiritual growth.

Sadly, most churches miss this truth.

They are not simple. They have not designed a simple process for discipleship. They have not structured their church around the process of spiritual transformation. And they are making little impact.

These churches need an extreme makeover. They desperately need a new design for church ministry.

We make these statements with confidence because our research indicates that the simple church strategy is effective. A simple process makes a major difference. The research is convincing.

We need to go back to the beginning, before we became convinced. We need to walk you through how we became advocates for a simple church strategy. Here is how the project was launched and unfolded.

Launching the Project

Two events led to the launch of this extensive research project.

First, as we interacted with vibrant and growing churches, we observed that these churches had a clear process for discipleship. They were streamlined and simple. Conversely, the struggling churches we observed had no clear process. They were complex and cluttered with programs.

We had a hunch.

And this was a hunch based on keen observation, not just a random feeling after dinner. It appeared that there was a relationship between being simple and being effective. Simple seemed to be working, but we had not yet tested it. We decided to put our observation through methodological research.

Second, we continually heard a cry for help from church leaders. Many feel bombarded and overwhelmed. Bombarded with models, programs, and new ideas. Overwhelmed with the busyness and the burden of pulling everything together. They are tired and restless.

Perhaps you are as well.

We saw a simple church design as a solution, and we wanted to advocate it. We wanted to offer it but could not do so without first testing it.

Our observations combined with our burden to offer tangible help to church leaders pulled us into this project. We began an extensive research project involving countless hours of work, the expertise and insight of seasoned church leaders, the processing of data by researchers, and hundreds of conversations with church leaders.

Here is how the research project unfolded.

The Research Phase

We wanted to discover whether there was a relationship between being simple and being effective. So we set out to explore the relationship between a simple church process and the vitality of a church.

We were tempted to adopt a case study approach to our research project. Tempted because it would have been the easy route. With a case study method, several churches are observed, and conclusions are made based on those observations. The case study approach is respected among researchers, but the approach greatly limits the applications that can be made to other churches. So we abandoned that idea.

Instead, we evaluated hundreds of churches so that we could apply the research on a broader scale.

In order to evaluate hundreds of churches, we created a survey that would measure the process design of a local church. We identified several vibrant churches that had a simple process. We studied these churches and concluded that each church had four key elements: clarity, movement, alignment, and focus.

We then assembled a team of seasoned church leaders to develop the survey based on the four key elements. The team consisted of pastors, church planters, denominational leaders, seminary professors, and church consultants. We called the survey the Process Design Survey. It measures how simple the process design of a local church is. It also measures how strongly a church excels in the four key elements.

While we do not claim inerrancy on this survey, the team was strongly united on the items that should be included in the survey. We jokingly refer to the conclave as the Council of Simple because agreement was so strong. It was amazing because the team was filled with strong leaders from a myriad of backgrounds. It was beautiful.

The survey was then tested with a group of churches to be sure it was consistent and reliable. It proved to be highly so. In fact, the survey proved reliable throughout the entire project. If you like stats, the Chronbach Alpha Index on the survey was .97. In case you are wondering, that is good. Most researchers consider .80 to be sufficient. A 1.0 is perfect. A .97 is great when you are using a new survey.

After the Process Design Survey was completed, we brought church leaders through the survey. Churches from several different evangelical denominations were included in the study. Churches from all over the United States participated, with representation from thirty-seven different states. The churches varied in size, style, type of setting, and years in existence.

The research on these churches took place in two stages.

In the first stage we had two groups complete the survey. The first group consisted of growing and healthy churches. These churches had grown 5 percent a year for three consecutive years. Few churches do that. Sadly, less than 2 percent of all churches in America experience that type of consistent growth.

The second group was the comparison group, churches that were not thriving. These churches had not grown or had declined over the same three-year period.

In the first stage 319 churches participated in the study. There were 166 from the vibrant/growing group and 153 from the comparison group. The results were greater than we imagined they would be. The vibrant churches scored much higher than the comparison churches. They proved to be simpler.

We conducted a second stage of the project with another sample. We wanted to confirm the results with another group.

This really was not necessary.

We already had enough data. It was statistically sound. Our statistician assured us we had found something "highly significant." We could have started writing, speaking, and preaching simple. It was already convincing.

We just wanted to be sure. We were about to make some big claims and recommendations. Telling complex churches to be simple would be revolutionary. Telling complex and cluttered churches they need an extreme makeover feels like accepting a double-dog dare. It is exciting, but we wanted to be doubly sure before we launched into this.

In the second stage of the research, eighty-eight churches participated. There were forty-four growing/vibrant churches and forty-four comparison churches. We applied the same criteria to the second phase of research as we had to the first. The results were even greater.

It was time for us to accept the double-dog dare.

It is time for churches to get an extreme makeover.

It is time to be simple.

The Results

The Process Design Survey has a range of one hundred points. The highest possible score is 120 and the lowest is 20. The survey and the scale were designed to measure how simple a local church is. The higher a church scored, the more simple the church.

During the first phase of the research, the mean (average) score for the vibrant/growing churches was eighty-five. The comparison churches scored an average of sixty-nine. During phase one, the vibrant churches scored 16 percent scale points higher than the comparison churches.

The results of phase two were similar and even more convincing. The vibrant/growing churches compiled an average score of eighty-seven, while the comparison churches scored an average of sixty-two. The vibrant churches scored 25 percent scale points higher than the comparison churches.

Here is the language researchers use of these results: "There is a highly significant relationship between a simple church design and the growth and vitality of a local church." The language that statisticians use for these results is even less enjoyable to read: "The results from the t tests and the correlating p values indicate that there is a highly statistically significant relationship between a simple church design and the growth and vitality of a local church."

While that information is important, we do not want to bore you with this language. We do not want to make these results complex or complicated. That would be painfully ironic since this book is about being simple.

So here is the practical language: In general, churches that are vibrant and growing are simple. The vibrant churches are much more simple than the comparison churches.

A simple church strategy is effective.

The vibrant church leaders proved to be expert designers. They have designed a straightforward and strategic ministry process. Not only did these churches score higher on the overall survey, but they also scored higher on each of the four simple church elements.

The four elements are critical to designing a simple ministry process. All four of the elements are necessary in a simple church design. The research also shows that the four elements are related to one another. In other words, it is hard to have one without the others.

So here is the expanded definition:

A simple church is designed around a straightforward and strategic process that moves people through the stages of spiritual growth. The leadership and the church are clear about the process (clarity) and are committed to executing it. The process flows logically (movement) and is implemented in each area of the church (alignment). The church abandons everything that is not in the process (focus).

Clarity. Movement. Alignment. Focus. All are necessary. The flow is simple, something like this:

Clarity ➻ Movement ➻ Alignment ➻ Focus

As you consider your ministry process, you must consider all four elements. Perhaps your church process needs some minor tweaking and decorating. Perhaps your church does not have a process. And perhaps your church is in need of an extreme makeover.

Regardless of your situation, as you design or redesign your ministry, these four elements should be on the forefront of your mind. Consider them to be essential designing tips.

Designing Tips

The *Extreme Makeover: Home Edition* design team is amazing to watch in action. They are expert designers and expert builders. Remember, you are called to be more than a programmer. You are to be an expert builder (1 Cor. 3:10).

The design team does more than come up with neat concepts. They are also able to execute. They design *and* implement. They are able to pull all the pieces together to create a great end result.

Their design process contains the same four elements we discovered in our research of simple churches: clarity, movement, alignment, and focus.

They begin with clarity. They first design an overall concept for the home and ensure everyone gets it. This step involves evaluating the present conditions of the home and the needs of the family. The design team sits around a table and engages in some robust discussion about the floor plan and footprint of the home.

They stare at the present blueprints. They dream. They discuss with passion what the house could be. Sometimes, they decide to tweak. Other times the house must come down.

Regardless of how they get there, they finally walk away with a clear plan, a blueprint. They know where they are headed. They pile their hands on top of one another and go for it. You feel like you're watching a team leave the locker room. In a very real way, you are.

The design team also sets up the project in sequential steps so it flows smoothly (movement). The project must move. For them, the project has to flow smoothly because of the time crunch. No time can be wasted. The next group of volunteers or the next vendor must be lined up and ready to go. The efficiency is impressive. And efficiency does not happen without sequence or movement.

The design team also masters alignment. They wisely place all of their resources and volunteers around their design process. Materials and volunteers are strategically placed. Volunteers and equipment are coordinated based on the sequence of the project.

The design team stays completely focused on the task. They cheer one another on. They remind one another why they are at that particular house. They keep their eyes on the goal, the end result. They manage their own passion. They monitor their own commitment.

Clarity, movement, alignment, and focus are all necessary to the design team. Without them, they would be unable to distribute grace to a family. All four elements enable them to design and build a great home.

Our calling is even greater.

Homes are temporal. Lives are eternal.

We are not designing buildings but ministries where people will be impacted by the grace of God. While ultimately Christ builds His church (Matt. 16:18), we are partners with Him. We may enjoy the honor of participating with Him in designing a ministry that transforms people.

According to our research, these four elements are critical in a ministry process that contributes to a vibrant church. These four elements enable leaders to have a simple church. Clarity, movement, alignment, and focus will be discussed in detail in upcoming chapters, but following is an overview.

Clarity

Clarity is *the ability of the process to be communicated and understood by the people.* A clear process has ability. It has the ability to be easily communicated and understood. Clarity involves certainty, and it eliminates confusion. For a church to be simple, the process must have a high degree of clarity.

Clarity and simplicity go hand in hand. They are close friends.

A process that has clarity is clearly defined. The leadership and the people know exactly how the church is structured to move people toward spiritual growth. The *how* is clear. The process (the *how*) is discussed, taught, and illustrated. And the people get it.

Some churches are not clear on a ministry process because they do not have one. Others have one, but it is too complex. It is too complicated, too long, or too confusing. The process is ineffective because it cannot be understood. Without understanding, commitment wanes.

Understanding always precedes commitment.

If people are to embrace and participate in the ministry process, they must be able to internalize it. To internalize the process, they must first grasp it. Clarity is thus absolutely essential.

Before the process can be clear to the people in the church, it must first be clear to the leaders. This point is where the breakdown most often occurs. As with Pastor Rush in chapter 1 and First Church in chapter 2, church leaders often stumble through an explanation of a ministry process.

Instead of clarity, there is often stuttering.

If leaders are not clear, the people will not grasp the ministry process. If leaders have a difficult time discussing and teaching the ministry process, it lacks clarity. And if the process lacks clarity, the process is not simple.

A lack of clarity ultimately leads to confusion and complexity because there is no coherent direction. When there is no direction, people assume a direction or invent one. The church then moves aimlessly and off course. And there is no course in which to return.

Simple churches have a course in which to return. They possess a clearly defined process. They are certain about *how* God has led them to make disciples. Their ministry process is a reflection of this certainty.

To be simple, a church must be clear. The results of the research confirm the necessity of clarity.

The clarity section on the Process Design Survey has a range of twenty-four points. The highest possible score is thirty and the lowest is six. The higher the score, the clearer the process.

During phase one of the research, the mean (average) score for the vibrant/growing churches was twenty. The comparison churches scored an average of fifteen. These scores mean that, in phase one, the vibrant churches scored 20 percent scale points higher than the comparison churches.

The results of the second research phase showed an even greater difference. Vibrant/growing churches scored an average of twenty, and the comparison churches scored an average of thirteen. In phase two, the vibrant churches scored 29 percent scale points higher than the comparison churches.

Simple churches have a crystal-clear process. They work hard to ensure everyone grasps it. Simple church leaders know their church's process and are able to articulate it to others with conviction. They are able to do so because they own the process.

Movement

Movement is *the sequential steps in the process that cause people to move to greater areas of commitment*. Movement is about flow. It is about assimilation. Movement is what causes a person to go to the next step.

Movement is the most difficult simple church element to understand; therefore, an illustration is in order.

In a relay race the most important part of the race are the handoffs. Four runners are on the same team, and each runner's speed is crucial but not nearly as crucial as the handoffs. Relay races are won or lost at the handoffs.

Sometimes the teams with the best runners lose, and teams with the best handoffs win. You have seen it. A team is out in the lead, and then someone drops the baton during a handoff. And the team loses.

The handoffs are that important.

Movement is about the handoffs. Movement is what happens in between the programs. Movement is *how* someone is *handed off* from one level of commitment to a greater level of commitment. How a church moves someone from a worship service to a small group is movement. How a church is designed to move a person from being an observer to being a contributor is movement.

Sadly, most churches are like poor relay teams. Instead of caring about the handoffs, they are preoccupied with the programs. They pay little attention to how people are moved to greater levels of commitment. They ignore what happens between the programs.

Simple churches pay attention to the handoffs. They have grasped the truth that assimilation effectiveness is more important than programmatic effectiveness. They know that as the flow of a process increases, so does the potential that people will progress through it. Simple church leaders design a ministry process where the programs are placed as tools along the process.

The vibrant churches we studied have a simple process that produces movement, a process that facilitates the handoffs. The programs in these churches are tools used to promote movement. The leaders focus on what happens in between the programs as much as they do the programs.

Our research confirms that movement is an essential design element in a simple church. According to the data, vibrant and growing churches have already recognized the importance of movement.

The movement section on the Process Design Survey has a range of twenty-four points. The highest possible score on the movement element is thirty, and the lowest is six. The higher the score, the greater the movement within the process.

During phase one of the research, the average score for the vibrant/growing churches was twenty-two. The comparison churches scored an average of seventeen. In phase one, the vibrant churches scored 21 percent scale points higher than the comparison churches.

The results of the second research phase showed an even greater difference. The vibrant/growing churches scored an average of twenty-two compared to an average of sixteen for the comparison churches. In phase two, the vibrant churches scored 25 percent scale points higher than the comparison churches.

Winning teams excel in the handoffs, and so do simple churches. They are experts in designing a simple process that produces movement.

To implement the movement element, church leaders must take a fresh look at the weekly church calendar and the regularly scheduled programs. All programs must be placed in sequential order along the ministry process. This is what creates movement in a ministry process.

Alignment

Alignment *is the arrangement of all ministries and staff around the same simple process.* Alignment to the process means that all ministry departments submit and attach themselves to the same overarching process.

Alignment ensures the entire church body is moving in the same direction, and in the same manner.

When a church is fully aligned, all ministries are operating from the same ministry blueprint. The ministries not only embrace the simple process, but they are engaged in it. Each ministry department mirrors the process in that particular area.

Without alignment, the church can be a multitude of sub-ministries. In this case each ministry has its own leaders who are only passionate about their specific ministry. They rarely identify with the entire church but are deeply committed to their own philosophy of ministry.

In a church that lacks alignment, everyone is competing for the same space, resources, volunteers, and time on the calendar.

In a church that lacks alignment, it does not feel like one body. It feels more like a building that houses a wide variety of ministries.

All churches naturally drift away from alignment.

Most of the times it is not addressed. The reasons vary. For one, it is painful to do so because committed people who have been around for a long time are passionate about their particular way of doing ministry. Sadly, they are more passionate for their area than for the church as a whole. Addressing misalignment also takes time and energy. It costs something to address it.

Unfortunately, it costs more not to address misalignment.

When misalignment on a car is not addressed, the results are damaging. Tires can blow out while driving. Damage to the wheels can occur. The same is true for a church. When misalignment is not addressed, there is damage.

Our research affirms that alignment is essential to being a simple church. Without alignment, complexity is certain.

The alignment section on the Process Design Survey has a range of twenty-four points. The highest possible score on the alignment element is thirty and the lowest is six. The higher the score, the greater the alignment around the process.

During phase one of the research, the average score for the vibrant/growing churches was twenty-two. The comparison churches scored an average of eighteen. In phase one, the vibrant churches scored 17 percent scale points higher than the comparison churches.

The results of the second research phase showed an even greater difference. The vibrant/growing churches scored an average of twenty-two compared to an average of sixteen for the comparison churches. In phase two, the vibrant churches scored 25 percent scale points higher than the comparison churches.

Our research indicates that simple churches practice alignment. They intentionally fight the drift into misalignment. They insist that each staff member and each ministry embrace and execute their simple ministry process.

Focus

Focus is the *commitment to abandon everything that falls outside of the simple ministry process*. Focus most often means saying "no." Focus requires saying "yes" to the best and "no" to everything else.

While movement is the most difficult simple church element to understand, focus is also the most difficult element to implement. It takes deep conviction and guts. Focus does not make church leaders popular.

Simple churches have a clearly defined process. The process is designed to move people to higher levels of commitment, and it is implemented in each department of the church so there is alignment. Clarity, movement, and alignment are essential.

But these three elements are ineffective without focus.

Focus is the element that gives power and energy to clarity, movement, and alignment.

Without focus, the church becomes cluttered despite its process. Without focus the process is unrecognizable because so many other programs and events surround it. Without focus, the process is buried somewhere underneath a myriad of special events and activities.

Simple churches abandon all that is outside of the simple process because it threatens to steal attention and energy from what has been determined as necessary. Events, activities, and programs outside the process cause people to move in multiple directions. A lack of focus leads to scattering.

Simple church leaders are focused people. They are not mean, and they don't necessarily like saying "no." They are just committed to the simple process that God has given that particular church.

Simple church leaders ask the difficult questions. They want to be sure something will fit neatly in the ministry process before it is implemented. They seek to funnel new ideas into their ministry process instead of beginning new paradigms.

They view everything through the lens of the simple process. They admittedly have blinders on. They are sometimes accused of being narrow-minded. They focus on being simple.

According to our research, their focus is justified.

The focus section on the Process Design Survey has a range of twenty-four points. The highest possible score on the focus element is thirty and the lowest is six. The higher the score, the more focused the church is on the process.

During phase one of the research, the mean (average) score for the vibrant/growing churches was twenty-two. The comparison churches scored an average of eighteen. In phase one, the vibrant churches scored 17 percent scale points higher than the comparison churches.

The results of the second research phase showed an even greater difference. The vibrant/growing churches scored an average of twenty-two compared to an average of seventeen for the comparison churches. In phase two, the vibrant churches scored 21 percent scale points higher than the comparison churches.

Simple churches have focus. Vibrant and growing churches are much more focused than the comparison churches. While focus is necessary, it is not easy. Even after years of establishing a simple ministry process, the focus element will be tested and questioned. Church leaders must have the single-mindedness of the apostle Paul who said, "One thing I do" (Phil. 3:13).

Hezekiah and Makeovers

Hezekiah was a revolutionary for simple. He was extremely focused. He was against cluttered spiritual lives. Evidently God liked this characteristic about him because 2 Kings 18:3 indicates that Hezekiah did what "was right in the LORD's sight."

He returned God's people to the Lord. He brought them through an extreme makeover. He got rid of some things. First, he removed the high places and cut down the Asherah poles (2 Kings 18:4). Basically, he threw out the altars that were set up to make-believe gods. He took out the godless clutter that had been competing for the attention and the affection of the people.

Most church leaders are willing to do that. This move was surely understood and embraced by even the nominal God worshippers in Hezekiah's day. They would expect the leader to insist that the people worship God.

Eliminating pagan idols is one thing, but what Hezekiah did next was controversial. Many church leaders would struggle to emulate his next move. Surely, people in his day struggled with this next change.

He broke the bronze snake that Moses had made—on purpose.

He did not just drop it and claim it was an accident. He broke it into pieces. The mental picture of a baseball player breaking a bat over his knee comes close. Yes, it was the special and sacred snake. The snake that was crafted and held by Moses. The snake that God had instructed Moses to make. The snake that was the source of salvation for the people from their snakebites (Num. 21:6–8).

He got rid of it because it was clutter. It was clutter because the people worshipped it. It took attention away from the real Savior. Bronze was worshipped. A fake snake was adored. What was once a good thing became an idol. It got in the way of their worship of God. The tool for worship became the object of worship.

In many churches the original tools for life change have created too much clutter. Instead of uniting, they divide focus. The programs have become ends in themselves.

Most churches need an extreme makeover and a modern-day Hezekiah.

For Hezekiah, eliminating the bronze snake was most likely not a popular decision, especially with the religious crowd steeped deep in tradition. Most extreme makeovers involving God's people are difficult.

Hezekiah did something that was probably perceived as being on the edge of sanity. It was a radical move. And this pleased God. In fact, there was no king like him before or after his time (2 Kings 18:5).

The church needs some modern-day Hezekiahs.

Would the next Hezekiah please begin the extreme makeover?

Hans Hofmann and Makeovers

Hans Hofmann was another revolutionary for simple.

He was born in Bavaria in the late 1800s. He became an artist and a teacher of other great artists. He learned from legends such as Picasso and Braque. He started and taught art at the Hans Hofmann School of Fine Arts in Manhattan. Hofmann even schooled Robert DeNiro's father in the craft.

Hofmann once indicated that if you want the necessary to stand out, you have to get rid of the unnecessary.

There are a lot of things that are unnecessary in most churches. It is tempting to leave these things alone, to avoid the struggle of an extreme makeover. However, the unnecessary often gets in the way of the necessary. The unnecessary divides attention, resources, and time. The unnecessary can hide the necessary.

And churches need the necessary to stand out.

To be simple you have to eliminate the unnecessary. Most of the things you eliminate will be good things. They were started with a passionate leader and a perceived or real need.

The key is to choose the best. Eliminate the unnecessary and keep the best. "And I pray this: . . . that you can determine what really matters" (Phil. 1:9–10).

So how many churches have successfully become simple churches? Not many at this point. But there is momentum in this simple church revolution. Join us in the next chapter as we visit three of these revolutionary churches.

Group Discussion Questions

1. What is our church's ministry process?
2. Is our process clear? Does it have clarity?
3. Does our process effectively move people toward greater levels of commitment?
4. Is our process implemented in all areas of our church? Are we aligned around our process?
5. How focused is our church?
6. What would Hezekiah think of our church?

FOUR

Three Simple Stories

*Upon this rock I will build My church; and the gates of
Hades will not overpower it.*
~ JESUS, MATTHEW 16:18 NASB

Clarity ➤➤ Movement ➤➤ Alignment ➤➤ Focus

There is an interesting conversation in Matthew 16. If you jump into the conversation, you will find Jesus asking His disciples who people say that He is. It is a simple question. It is not complicated. It is straight and to the point.

And it is a question that is not asked frequently. He does not ask what people are saying about Him. He does not ask if people are saying He is a nice guy or a great speaker. His question is different. He asks, "*Who* do people say that the Son of Man is?" (v. 13). The disciples tell Him that some people are saying He is John the Baptist. Others are saying He is Elijah.

Jesus then asks the disciples the same question. He wants to know what they think. "Who do you say that I am?" (v. 15).

Peter, of course, speaks for the entire group. He replies, "You are the Messiah, the Son of the living God" (v. 16).

Jesus loves his response. He calls Peter blessed. The words Peter spoke came not from man but from God. Jesus then says, "Upon this rock I will build My church; and the gates of Hades will not overpower it" (Matt. 16:18 NASB).

The gates of hades will not overcome it. Hell will not be able to hold back the church. Jesus says he is going to unleash a movement that will be so powerful and intense that it will be unstoppable. This movement is the church. It is not an institution, a building, a program, a creed, or a doctrinal statement. This movement is alive and growing. This movement is people. Jesus started the church, and the gates of hell will not be able to contain it.

The Theology of Gates

So that his in-laws would be somewhat comfortable with their daughter living in Miami, Eric bought a house in a gated community. After all, Miami is not known as the safest place to live. *Miami Vice* and now *CSI Miami* do not help the perception. So Eric was excited to tell his in-laws that he was doing all that he could to protect their daughter. He lives in a gated community south of Miami.

At least that is what the brochure said when he bought the house.

It turns out the gate is just a piece of PVC pipe attached to a mechanical device. That's it. In the two and a half years Eric has lived in the house, the gate has been up approximately forty-one hours.

The demise of the gate is pretty simple. People who did not receive the clicker in the mail decided to run through the gate. The painted piece of PVC pipe was no match for the cars. The gate cracked off. For a few weeks the homeowners association paid a company to fix the gate. Then someone else would run through the gate. Eventually the homeowners association decided to stop paying.

So now the gate/PVC pipe lies on the ground. It is just beneath the sign that points people to the gated community. The gate could not stop the traffic. It could not overcome the power of cars. It was pathetic in comparison.

The gates of hell are the same way. They are powerless to contain the movement of the gospel. Jesus started the movement, and hell cannot contain it.

There is another thing about gates. They are always defensive. They protect. They guard. But they never attack. The gate lying next to the sign in Eric's neighborhood has never attacked Eric despite all that he has said about it. The gate is inept.

Gates are never on offense. Only defense. Hell is always on defense. However, the movement of the church is never on defense. Only offense. The church always has the ball. There are no defenders on the squad.

This is good news. Victory is guaranteed.

The question is not whether we are going to win or not. Our victory celebration has already been determined. Christ has promised it. We win in the end. In fact, the enemy never gets the ball. The kingdom of darkness is stuck on defense. And we are on perpetual offense.

Even the more inept team could win if the other team never played offense. It may take some time, but they would win. Eventually.

The question is, how much will we win by? How big of a dent in the gates of hell will we make? Will we run up the score? Will we push the movement of the gospel forcefully through the gates of hell?

In this chapter you will encounter three simple stories. These are stories of simple churches that are running up the score. These churches are making a big dent in the kingdom of darkness. God is using these churches to push back the enemy.

While the research project focused on hundreds of churches, we wanted to give you the story of several simple churches. Churches of varying size and setting have been selected. First, you will hear the story of a rural church of three hundred people. Next you will hear the story of a church in one of the most unchurched American cities. Finally, you will encounter one of the fastest-growing churches in American history.

May the gates of hell lie damaged on the ground. Right next to that PVC pipe.

Story 1: Immanuel

There are a lot of Immanuel churches. There is probably one in your community. Some spell it with an *E* and some spell it with an *I*. And some people are really proud of how they spell it.

This story is about Immanuel Baptist Church in Glasgow, Kentucky. Glasgow is a city of sixteen thousand people located in Barren County. Barren County has forty thousand residents. Glasgow is the buckle of the Bible Belt. The town is dry. There are more than one hundred churches listed on the city Web site.

People in Glasgow enjoy the pace of life and the Southern hospitality. There is virtually no crime, and the schools are well respected. Traffic is minimal unless you get stuck behind an old

pickup truck going thirty-five miles an hour. The land is beautiful and plentiful. People trust their neighbors. Life is good.

In most rural Bible-belt towns, there are churches on every
corner. Nearly everyone can claim membership in some church,
even if they have not been in years. Many of the churches are
struggling. Rarely are new people brought to Christ. Every few
years one church has some problems, and another church three
blocks over gets some new members.

The Bible-belt culture is the same in Glasgow. Yet Immanuel
is different. God is using Immanuel to push back the gates
of hell.

Immanuel Baptist Church is vibrant. Alive. And growing.
In the last two years the church has doubled in attendance from
150 to more than three hundred. Guests are coming regularly.
Many people have been converted to the faith. The church bap-
tizes people regularly. People are growing and serving.

Immanuel is also different because Immanuel is simple.
The complexity that plagues many rural churches does not
exist. Instead Immanuel has a simple process that guides their
ministry.

Clarity at Immanuel

Tony Cecil is the pastor of Immanuel Baptist Church. He is
thirty-three years old, and Immanuel is his first church to serve
as senior pastor. When Tony arrived in Glasgow, he knew the
church needed a simple process for discipleship. He commented,

As a twenty-nine-year old, first-time senior pastor,
I struggled with the dysfunction and chaos that char-
acterized the churches I had encountered. By the grace
of God, through personal study and conversations with
friends, I began to see the importance of embracing and
implementing a strategic process for making disciples.

Tony gathered a group of godly leaders in his church. They sought to define what kind of disciple they would seek to make at Immanuel. They concluded that fully committed believers would be intimate with God and other Christians, people who grow in their faith, and are servants in the kingdom of God.

Tony and the group chose to describe their discipleship focus as a process. They call it *Connecting, Growing, Serving*. First, Immanuel seeks to connect people to God and others. They desire to see people become "connecting believers." Next they challenge "connecting believers" to become "growing believers" by engaging in opportunities for deeper spiritual growth. Finally, the process ends with "growing believers" committing to become "serving believers."

Movement at Immanuel

To promote movement though the process, Immanuel has placed their weekly programs at key points along their process. They use their Sunday morning worship services to make "connecting believers." The worship service is designed to bring people into a relationship with God and other Christians.

After someone comes to the worship service, the person is encouraged to plug into an adult Bible fellowship. Immanuel offers adult Bible fellowships on Sunday mornings to make "growing believers."

The process does not end there. Once an adult attends an adult Bible fellowship, the person is challenged to join a smaller group. These smaller groups are designed to help people become "serving believers." Each adult Bible fellowship is made up of several smaller groups. These groups are serving teams, and they do ministry together either in the community or in the church.

Immanuel strategically moves adults from worship services to Bible fellowships to small groups. By moving people from program to program, people naturally progress through the simple process.

Movement is intentional at Immanuel. For example, the content of the adult Bible fellowships coincides with the message in the worship service. Tony writes what he calls "coordinates" each week that supplement his message. The Bible fellowship leaders use these coordinates as curriculum. Tony is able to invite the people at the worship service to attend a Bible fellowship "to get more information and go deeper."

People are intentionally moved from the "connecting believer" level to the "growing believer" level. There is a clear overlap between the worship service and the next step. The overlap promotes movement. Without an overlap, people fall through the cracks.

To move people from Adult Bible Fellowships (ABF) to serving groups, Tony and the ABF leaders decided to link the small serving groups to the ABFs. When someone goes to an ABF, they are immediately given the opportunity to plug into a small serving group. There is no space between the programs. Movement occurs easily.

Alignment at Immanuel

Since Immanuel is not a large church, there is not a myriad of ministries to align. The primary ministries at Immanuel are the age-specific ministries to children and teenagers. Both the children's and the youth ministry use the same simple process: *connect, grow, serve.*

The students have a weekly *connect* program designed to bring teenagers into a relationship with Christ. They use small groups to grow teenagers deeper, and they have ministry groups to engage students in service. The children have a weekly *connect* program and another weekly *grow* program.

Everyone uses the same terminology. Connect. Grow. Serve. Simple. It is woven into every part of the church. The people in the congregation hear it all the time.

Focus at Immanuel

Immanuel Baptist Church has a simple process that is clearly defined, moves people, and is implemented throughout the church. They have chosen to focus all of their energy and resources on this simple process. Because of their focus, they have been able to place all of their financial resources on the programs within the ministry process.

Some would think this focus would hamper the vitality of the church. In rural Bible-belt towns, churches are often known for the amount of special events they do. Immanuel goes against the culture. They are a part of the simple revolution. Tony remarked:

The irony is that we have actually grown numerically and spiritually by doing fewer programs and special events, choosing instead to focus our attention on moving people with various levels of commitment to deeper levels of commitment.

Fringe Benefits at Immanuel

We encountered this great church in the research phase of the project. Few churches experience the growth that Immanuel has seen. It has been explosive, not incremental. This church breaks all the rules. They are growing by reaching new people in a city that is not experiencing a population increase and is full of other churches. It is truly a God thing.

Designing a simple process for church ministry has made a major difference at Immanuel Baptist Church. We asked Tony to list some of the benefits to being a simple church. Following is what he shared:

• *Increased Morale.* Morale has improved by actually defining the Great Commission in the form of a simple disciple-making process. This reality seems to stem from people understanding how we propose to make disciples, rather than just being told that we need to make disciples.

• *Urgency.* There is an ever-increasing sense of urgency in moving people into spiritual maturity and ministry, rather than just seeing them converted.

• *Spiritual Growth.* Though hard to measure, we have seen believers grow and mature before our eyes. The process not only shows people where they are but also where they need to go next. As a result, people have become proactive in their own spiritual development. Personal commitments to Bible study and small group involvement have increased steadily. More individuals are sharing their faith; more people are inviting their friends to worship and small groups.

• *Conversions.* We've seen a significant increase in adult conversions and baptisms. Our ministry process has resulted in adults being more proactive in inviting their friends to the appropriate venues that are geared toward connecting people to Jesus Christ and other Christians. This process has also resulted in adults sensing a need to make a greater commitment to Christ by learning how to share their faith with their friends and family members. Before developing our process, our church had baptized two adults in the first eighteen months of my ministry. Since we have developed our process, we are on target to baptize forty people each year. This number still falls short of what we desire in terms of evangelism, but for us it's big-time improvement.

• **Stewardship.** Our financial situation has improved drastically by eliminating programs and ministries that do not contribute to our overall process. I've also seen that it's easier to eliminate programs after people have committed themselves to the congregational process.

• **Unity.** As we've experienced some short-term successes, our overall unity has been strengthened. We're becoming a closer family by agreeing on the process and consolidating our efforts around fulfilling it.

Story 2: Christ Fellowship

Until one year ago Christ Fellowship in Miami was First Baptist Church of Perrine. The community name changed to Palmetto Bay, and God led the church to a new name. Christ Fellowship is a multicultural church consisting of more than seventy nationalities. Rick Blackwood is the senior pastor, and Eric serves as his executive pastor. Before coming to LifeWay Thom consulted with the church. He believes Rick is one of the most humble large church pastors he has ever interacted with.

Miami may be in the South, but it is definitely not the Bible Belt. It is a city filled with people from all over the world in desperate need of the grace of God. Many churches struggle in Miami. Many pastors struggle in Miami. It is not an easy place to do ministry. Church and God are, at best, afterthoughts to the majority of people.

Christ Fellowship is eighty-nine years old. It is a church with a great history and tradition. In the last forty-five years, only two senior pastors have led the church. Often in churches with rich history, change is the most difficult. People see no reason to change. Things are fine as they are. There are a lot of programs and events, and most people are happy. The status quo is comfortable.

However, at Christ Fellowship, God assembled a team of pastors and leaders who were not satisfied. They believed God wanted to do more. They were convinced the gates of hell needed to be run through.

Several years ago the pastors at Christ Fellowship began evaluating the ministry. They sought to define the kind of disciple their church was seeking to make. God impressed on their hearts to focus people on four things: an intimate relationship with God, community with others, serving, and influencing nonbelievers. The vision for this kind of disciple gripped the staff.

They committed to these four aspects of discipleship. They committed to streamline, to become simple. Their commitment has been rewarding. The church is continually growing and seeing people, specifically adults, come to know Christ. People are growing in their faith and plugging into service opportunities.

Clarity at Christ Fellowship

While those four aspects of discipleship captivated the staff, they also knew discipleship was a process. They worked hard to craft a statement that would encompass both the process nature of discipleship and those four aspects. Like many churches they had vision, purpose, strategy, and mission statements. It was too much, too confusing.

They committed to one statement that would feature their simple process: Connect to God, others, ministry, and the lost. Discipleship includes being intimate with God (connect to God), living in community with other believers (connect to others), serving the body of Christ (connect to ministry), and sharing the gospel (connect to the lost).

The purpose at Christ Fellowship is a process. First, someone gets connected to God. That is the most basic and essential aspect of discipleship, but it does not end there. Next, the person gets connected to others. After loving God and others, the natural result is to minister to people. Finally, the person is living a life fully surrendered to God where evangelism is the overflow of this dynamic relationship.

The process has taken center stage in staff meetings and volunteer leadership meetings. It is preached with clarity and conviction from the pulpit. The worship folder and other key communication pieces explain it. The staff discusses the process and measures how people are progressing through it. All staff members, including administrative assistants, are expected to be able to communicate the process to others.

Movement at Christ Fellowship

The leaders at Christ Fellowship knew the process would be just another statement unless it was reflected in their weekly programming. The process would be just words if the programs did not become tools to move people through the process. The process and the programs have to be friends. They must complement each other.

So the staff discussed what the best programs were for each level of the process, and they committed to placing those programs in sequential order along the process. In other words, they decided to set up the weekly programs so people could easily move through the process simply by moving from one program to the next.

The first step in the process is to *connect to God*. During the weekend worship services people are able to begin or deepen their relationship with Christ. Through engaging worship and a biblical message, people are thrust into an environment where a growing and intimate relationship with God is the primary concern. Many guests also attend the worship services each week, so it makes sense that this would be the first program in the process.

The second step in the process is to *connect to others*, and the staff concluded that small groups best accomplish relational connection and interdependence. People may go to a weekend service faithfully, but if they never connect to a small group, their spiritual growth stagnates. And they are not really known. Small groups are offered on Sunday morning, Wednesday nights, and in homes during the week.

The third step in the process is to *connect to ministry*, and Christ Fellowship utilizes ministry teams to provide service opportunities for people. People experience God working through them as they minister to others in tangible ways. People are challenged to join a team that is engaged in ministry they are passionate about.

The final step in the process is to *connect to the lost*. At Christ Fellowship, this step is not a program but a relational lifestyle. People are challenged to invite friends and families to church. The church family is challenged not only to go through the process themselves but also to bring others through it. When someone is first brought to a weekend service, the process for that person begins.

Since the last step in the process is not a program, people are challenged to do three things a week at Christ Fellowship. Come to a worship service, be in a small group, and serve in a ministry. Simple. These expectations are stated clearly to people in the church. At the new member's class, people are told they should not join if they are not planning to move through the process.

To facilitate movement to small groups, small groups are promoted in the worship services. The church also frequently offers six-week small group series based on the worship service series. People are encouraged to join or start a group for the duration of the short-term series. This process has moved hundreds of people to small groups.

To facilitate movement to ministry, people are challenged to test-drive a ministry. A test-drive is an opportunity to serve with a ministry team for one serving session. They can experiment without any pressure to join the team. After the test-drive they debrief with the leader of the ministry and are given an opportunity to continue serving or to try another ministry team.

Alignment at Christ Fellowship

Alignment is evident at Christ Fellowship. The children's, middle school, high school, and young adult departments have the same process. You guessed it: Connect to God, others, ministry, and the lost. The staff is on the same page and moving in the same direction. The entire church is aligned around the same focus.

Children, middle school, and high school ministries provide their own *Connect to God* worship experience. They are offered every time an adult worship service occurs. Each age-specific department also offers small groups on Wednesday nights to connect their group to others. Each department also provides ministry opportunities for their specific age groups.

Focus at Christ Fellowship

Once the staff committed wholeheartedly to the process of connecting people to God, others, ministry, and the lost, difficult decisions had to be made. Eliminating programs that did not fit became necessary to maximize the impact of the process.

Over a two-year period, the churchwide Sunday night worship service was eliminated. And home groups, Sunday school classes, and Wednesday night discipleship groups were combined into one small-group strategy. All groups were placed under the same leadership and philosophy. These two changes made it easier for people to move through the process. People are now challenged to come to one service and one small group a week.

The extra programs are what business consultants refer to as nonvalue-adding work. They did not add value to the process. The extra programs actually competed with the process because people were less likely to plug into a small group and a ministry. People only have so much available time, and the leaders decided to free up time slots for people to be able to connect to the essential programs in the process.

In order to bring greater focus, even popular programs were altered or eliminated at Christ Fellowship.

One of the most popular programs in the church was known as the "Friday Night Open Rec" for students. It was free burgers, games, and basketball. Every Friday night it drew three hundred to four hundred students. While it was successful, it was unclear how it fit in the process.

The gospel was not shared at this event, and it was not the entry point into the student ministry, so it could not be classified as a "Connect to God" program. The student pastors could

not manage this weekly event and then provide another exciting "Connect to God" program during the weekend services.
Their attention would be divided. Also, the students would be
inviting friends to a program that was not in the process instead
of bringing them to one that is.

Friday Nights were cancelled. The program was reestab-
lished after the Saturday night service as a way to engage more
kids in the student "Connect to God" program. By placing the
food and games on top of the Saturday night service, more kids
are now in a student worship service.

Another popular program that was altered was the special
Christmas Eve services. Like many churches Christ Fellowship
offered specific Christmas Eve services each year. Many people who rarely come to church attended the Christmas Eve
services, but the services were completely different from the
weekend services. People never got a taste of what takes place
at the regular weekend services. The Christmas Eve services
failed to engage people in the simple process.

Active church members attended both the Christmas Eve
services and the regular weekend services. The worship staff
had to prepare two different types of services during the same
week, which lowered the level of excellence at both. This was
also poor stewardship of space because the same people were
coming multiple times instead of freeing up places for new
people.

Also, instead of inviting people to the weekend services,
church members were inviting friends and family to the
Christmas Eve services. These guests were never exposed to a
typical weekend service and were less likely to return.

To simplify things and expose as many people as possible
to a typical weekend service (the Connect to God program),
the staff decided to combine the Christmas Eve services with

the weekend services. Christ Fellowship now offers several identical weekend Christmas services. The elimination of the special program paid off immediately as the number of people who were exposed to a weekend service skyrocketed.

Story 3: Northpoint

While Immanuel Baptist Church and Christ Fellowship have transitioned to a simple church design, Northpoint Community church began that way.

Northpoint is the epitome of simple. They are pioneers.

Northpoint Community Church is located in Alpharetta, Georgia, just north of Atlanta. Andy Stanley is the founding and the senior pastor. While Andy grew up being exposed to complex churches, he chose to begin Northpoint with a commitment to simplicity. He believes that ministry naturally drifts toward complexity, that complexity just happens. Unfortunately, according to Stanley, "Complexity dilutes your potential for impact."[1]

To counteract complexity, the church has remained committed to their simple process. That commitment has pushed the gates of hell back. The church has grown from a handful of people to more than sixteen thousand in ten years. God has used the church to bring many people to faith and spiritual maturity. God is also using the church to challenge and encourage church leaders from all over the world.

Clarity at Northpoint

Northpoint Community Church has a clear process that is constantly referenced in the life of their church. They call it the "Foyer to the Kitchen." They seek to move people to *the kitchen* where people will be in community groups with others. They do so because they are convinced that life change best happens in that environment. So everything they do is designed to move people to the kitchen.

The metaphor comes from a time when Andy Stanley and his wife visited a church on a Sunday morning. As they were leaving, his wife commented that the church felt like being invited into someone's home and then ignored the rest of the time. Stanley became convinced that the church must be designed never to leave people alone. People must be moved to something.[2]

The church is designed to move people to greater levels of commitment and relationships. Their process begins with the *foyer*. Just as the foyer is used in someone's home to welcome guests, Northpoint refers to the first step in the process as their *foyer*.

The imagery of a home and the family continues throughout the process. The next step is the *living room*. After guests are made to feel welcome in the foyer, they are moved to the living room where relationships are built. Without the living room, people would remain in the foyer. There would be no place to go. Without the *living room* environment at Northpoint, people would not progress to the final step.

The final step in the process is the *kitchen*. In most homes the kitchen is where the most intimate conversations occur. It is where life happens together and where family discussions take place. At Northpoint the *kitchen* is the deepest level of commitment. It is where people are transformed in community with others. People are held accountable and spur one another on toward spiritual maturity.

Movement at Northpoint

The entire "Foyer to Kitchen" process at Northpoint Community Church is about movement. They resist the word *program* and use the words *steps* or *environments* instead. Steps are about movement. They are seeking to move people to the *kitchen* because they are convinced life change happens there. They only use steps that get people there.[3]

Northpoint has placed their environments/steps sequentially along this process to facilitate movement. Their *foyer* environment is their worship service, and it is the clear entrypoint for the church. People are encouraged to invest in the lives of nonbelievers and invite them to church; therefore, their weekend worship service is the program where guests are expected to be.[4]

Their *living room* environment is what they refer to as GroupLink. It is where people connect to one another relationally. GroupLink does not meet every week. It is offered at strategic times throughout the year. The focus is to get people to know one another. The intention is to use the GroupLink to move people to the kitchen/small groups.

Their *kitchen* environment is where people meet together in small groups for deep fellowship and Bible study. Andy claims their process is extremely simple because it seeks to move their people through these three environments. People are then challenged to bring others through the same process.

Movement is the trump card at Northpoint.

There are no environments at Northpoint where people stay forever. This is in stark contrast to churches where people sit in the same groups for decades. At Northpoint, people are continually moved to another step. Even when someone reaches the kitchen, movement is not complete. Small groups must start new small groups.

At Northpoint, all steps must take people somewhere. They must not be ends in themselves. They must move people toward the kitchen environment. If not, they harm the process.

Andy commented, "Every program must facilitate movement through the simple process. Anything that facilitates movement is a 'yes.' Anything that does not is a 'no.'"[5]

Alignment at Northpoint

Because the "Foyer to Kitchen" process is implemented at every level of the church, Northpoint enjoys the power of team alignment. Every ministry is on the same page and uses the same verbiage. And this alignment fosters unity. People are not fighting over the same space, resources, and leaders. Each ministry complements the others.

The goal of each department is to move people to the kitchen. According to family pastor Reggie Joiner, this process is so simple that it can be explained in a few minutes on a napkin. Each department understands the process and is committed to it. The process is the same for each area.

Their process could be drawn with three circles. The first circle is the largest. It is the foyer environment for each ministry. Every age-specific ministry at Northpoint has a foyer. The second circle is smaller. This circle represents the living room for each ministry. Each ministry department in the church also has a third circle, the smallest. This circle represents the kitchen. At every level of the church, ministry departments are seeking to move people from circle to circle through the process.[6]

Focus at Northpoint

If you go to Northpoint, you will be struck by how ministry is executed with excellence. Things are just done right. The culture of excellence permeates the entire church from the campus grounds to the greeters to children's and youth ministries. The worship services are inspiring and engaging.

The reason Northpoint is able to do things so well is because they have chosen to only do a few things.

The church has rejected the menu philosophy of ministry that encourages church leaders to offer huge menus of programs. It is no wonder ministry is done poorly in most churches. It is impossible to do things with excellence when energy and attention are divided. Reggie Joiner refers to these churches as ADD churches. They have an inability to focus.

At Northpoint, less really is more. They have done much less than most churches but have been able to accomplish much more.

Simplicity is not just lip service at Northpoint. They refuse to add programs or events that will distract people from the simple process that God has given them. Again, they began simple, so people are often shocked to learn what programs are not offered at Northpoint. Reggie Joiner writes:

> Many of our staff had previously been involved with churches that were program-heavy, and we know how quickly things could grow out of control. So we became tenacious about staying simple. In fact, you might be surprised at some of the things we do not do. For example, we don't have a Christian school, midweek services, men and women's ministries, a children's choir, adult Sunday school, Easter or Christmas Pageants, or a recreation ministry.[7]

Immanuel. Christ Fellowship. Northpoint—three different churches in different communities. Their worship styles are different. The makeup of their congregations is different. Their church government is different.

Yet each church is simple. Each church is vibrant. Each has a simple process that guides its ministry. And each church is pushing back the gates of hell.

How do the gates look in your community? We mean spiritually.

Is your church pushing the movement of the gospel forward? Are you putting dents in the kingdom of darkness? Are you running up the score?

Now What

You have been introduced to the simple revolution.

You have learned how people are responding to simple because life is so complex. You have gone on a consulting trip and seen a simple church and a complex church. You have learned the four major elements of the simple church through an overview of the research findings and an encounter with three simple churches.

Now it is time to get specific and practical.

In part 2, you will be guided through the four elements of a simple church. You will wrestle with and understand clarity, movement, alignment, and focus. You will see the significant research findings that cannot be ignored. And you will be given practical insight on how to implement all four of these critical elements.

You have been introduced to the simple revolution.

It is now time to become a simple church.

GROUP DISCUSSION QUESTIONS

1. Why is it much easier to begin as a simple church than it is to become one?
2. What is the relationship between focus and excellence in ministry?
3. What common factors exist in these three churches?

4. What differences emerge?
5. Of the four simple church elements—clarity, movement, alignment, and focus—which will be the most difficult to implement in our church? Why?
6. What does the movement of the gospel look like in our community?

PART 2

Becoming a Simple Church

FIVE

Clarity: Starting with a Ministry Blueprint

If anyone's work that he has built survives,
he will receive a reward.
~ THE APOSTLE PAUL, 1 CORINTHIANS 3:14

Clarity ➤➤ Movement ➤➤ Alignment➤➤ Focus

Congratulations, you are a builder.

Build lives. That is what ministry is all about. It is what you and your church are called to do. The apostle Paul gives specific instructions to church leaders:

And He personally gave some to be apostles, some prophets, some evangelists, some pastors and teachers, for the training of the saints in the work of ministry, to build up the body of Christ. (Eph. 4:11–12)

Ministry is done so that the body of Christ may be built up. The term Paul uses for "build up" is the Greek word *oikodome*.

It is a construction term. It paints the picture of building a house. Constructing lives is the calling.

This imagery runs throughout the New Testament. Believers are challenged to continue growing in the faith:

> Therefore as you have received Christ Jesus the Lord, walk in Him, rooted and built up in Him and established in the faith, just as you were taught, and overflowing with thankfulness. (Col. 2:6–7)

Notice the language. The term for *built up* is a present-tense participle. This indicates continuous action. The house is always being tweaked. The application is simple—building lives is active and ongoing. It is a process.

There is more. First Peter 2:5 and Ephesians 2:22 compare the expanding of the kingdom of God to the building of a house. As people come to faith in Christ, the spiritual house is expanded. A new addition is constantly being added.

In both senses you are called to partner with God in a great building project. You are to build the spiritual house by bringing people into a relationship with God. And you are to build the lives of individuals by helping them progress in the faith.

You are a builder.

According to the apostle Paul, you must take this role seriously (1 Cor. 3:14). You must be careful *how* you build. The *how* is important. It is and it always has been.

As a builder, you need some clear blueprints.

Blueprints are not blue anymore, but they are still as vital as ever.

Blueprints are essential when designing or building. They show not only what will be built but also *how* it will be built. They show in great detail how everything fits together.

Building without blueprints would be ridiculous. It is inconceivable. You would never trust a physical house to a builder without blueprints. A good builder doesn't just wing it. He begins with a clear plan, a clear design.

A builder comes to the table with more than a brochure.

Brochures are different from blueprints. Brochures show the finished product. They show what the house will look like. However, you could not build a house with a brochure. It would be insufficient. The brochure is pretty, but it is not clear.

Blueprints contain more depth. You could follow the blueprint and build a house.

Why would we attempt to build spiritual lives without a clear ministry blueprint? To build the lives of people effectively, you need a clear ministry process. You need a blueprint that has clarity. According to our data, there is a highly significant relationship between church vitality and the clarity of the process. Clarity is *the ability of the process to be communicated and understood by the people.*

You are a builder, and it is time to design a ministry blueprint. It is time to be sure you have a clear ministry process. In this chapter you will be given five keys to clarity. All five are essential and have been validated by our research.

If you want your process to be clear, you must define it, illustrate it, discuss it, and measure it. You must also constantly monitor the understanding of your people in regard to your process.

1: Define

According to our research, defining your ministry process is extremely important.

We asked vibrant church leaders and comparison church leaders to evaluate how clearly defined their ministry process is. We asked them to state their level of agreement with the following statement: "We have a clearly defined process for moving a person from salvation to spiritual maturity to significant ministry."

Of the vibrant churches, 53 percent of the church leaders agreed or strongly agreed that they have a clearly defined process. Of the comparison churches, 25 percent of the leaders agreed or strongly agreed.

Figure 1 illustrates this. Notice how the majority of the comparison churches are on the left side of the figure, while the majority of the vibrant churches are on the right. Vibrant churches are more than twice as likely than comparison churches to have a clearly defined process.

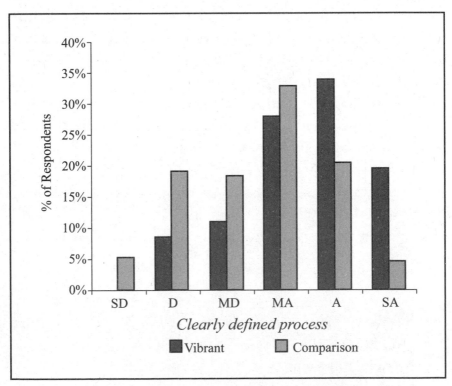

Figure 1. Respondents' level of agreement with having a clearly defined process

Note: SD = Strongly disagree; D = Disagree; MD = Moderately disagree;
MA = Moderately agree; A = Agree; SA = Strongly agree

So the beginning point is to define your process.

Without definition, people are uncertain about *how* the church is making disciples. Without definition, people are clueless about *how* the church is designed to bring people toward spiritual maturity. Without definition, there is room for ambiguity. Most churches are ambiguous about their ministry process, either because they do not have one or because it is loosely defined.

And where there is ambiguity, there is often confusion.

Several times in Miami, ambiguity has led to confusion for people who meet Eric's wife, who is especially tan from living in South Florida. She is often asked in Spanish, "Como té llama?" which means, "What is your name?"

Since she knows a little Spanish, she responds appropriately, "Kaye." Kaye is her name. But *Kaye* sounds like *que*. And *que* means "what?"

So the person will ask the question again in Spanish. This time, a little louder, "Como té llama?" And the person will get the same response. Usually after a few times of asking, the person gives up frustrated. For the Spanish-speaking person, the conversation feels like this:

"What is your name?"

"What."

"What is your name?"

"What."

You get the picture. The moment is filled with ambiguity. Multiple definitions for the same sounding word leads to confusion and frustration.

The same is true with defining a process for church ministry. If the process is not clearly defined so that everyone is speaking the same language, there is confusion and frustration.

If there is not one clearly defined *how*, people construct multiple interpretations on the direction of the church.

How's Your *How?*

Defining the process is formulating a strategy. It is agreeing to a blueprint. And this blueprint describes not only the kind of disciple that will be built but also *how*.

Church leaders must define more than the purpose (*the what*); they must also define the process (*the how*). Thom previously discovered in his research on evangelistically effective churches that effective churches have leaders who are clear about the purpose of the church.[1] This new research affirms that finding and also reveals that it is important to be clear about the ministry process.

Michael Hammer is a business consultant who meets with organizations about their processes. The cost to attend one of his two-day conferences is more than two thousand bucks a person (ouch). He believes that the process is more important than the purpose of a company because it is the process that makes everything work. It is the *how*. He points out that the people within any organization must know the process because they are integral to fulfilling it.[2]

The same is true for a church. People within a church must know the process because they are integral to fulfilling it.

Actually, the process is for them. It is designed for them, for everyone. The end result is their lives transformed. People are more likely to progress through the process if they know it. A clearly defined process encourages people to progress through it because they know the expectation. People cannot embrace the ambiguous.

How is your *how?* Do you have a process that is clearly defined? Following are three concepts to wrestle with as you begin to define a ministry process:

Determine what kind of disciple you wish to produce in your church. What do you want the people to *be?* Narrow this list down as much as possible. For example, Cross Church (chapter 2) decided that disciples at their church would be passionate lovers of God, servants in the kingdom of God, and connected in vibrant relationships to people.

Describe your purpose as a process. After you conclude what you desire people in your church or ministry to be, describe this in process terms. In other words, describe your purpose in sequential order. Process definition is much easier for church leaders if they describe their church purpose statement as a process.

Cross Church took their desires for disciples and placed them in sequential order: "Love God, love others, serve the world." Someone first commits to love God. The person then gets connected in vibrant relationships with others and finally expresses love for God and others by serving the world.

The leaders at Cross Church believe that spiritual growth is a process, and they describe the focus of their church in such terms. The order is important. It provides a clear blueprint for the leaders at Cross Church.

Decide how each weekly program is part of the process. Let's be honest; the programs and ministries are what people see. People forget the statements on the wall, but they know what programs you offer. Your programs say what is important to you; therefore, you must define how each program is used to produce the kinds of disciples God has called you to make.

The programs must specifically be defined how they will be used to move people through the process of spiritual transformation. Cross Church focuses their worship services on helping people love God. They use small groups to help people love others, and they challenge people to be on a ministry team so they can serve the world.

Your programs must be submissive to your ministry process. They are tools to facilitate the process of spiritual growth. Programs must work for your process, not the other way around.

Define your process, and then illustrate it.

2: Illustrate

According to our research, illustrating your process is vital. If you want your church members to see your simple process clearly, you must illustrate it.

Blueprints are visual. Can you imagine building a house without having the drawing to look at? Can you imagine constructing a building without having the blueprints on the table as discussions emerge?

We asked vibrant church leaders and comparison church leaders if they use an illustration or metaphor to help bring clarity to their process. We asked them to state their level of agreement with the following statement: "We have a visual illustration of our process."

Of the vibrant churches, 35 percent strongly agreed or agreed with the statement compared to 16 percent of the comparison churches. The percentage of vibrant church leaders who agreed or strongly agreed that their church has a visual illustration of their process was more than twice that of the comparison church leaders (Figure 2).

The majority of comparison churches admit that they do not illustrate their process. Over 70 percent of the comparison church leaders disagreed at some level that their church illustrates their process visually.

The data urges church leaders to choose a visual illustration to represent their simple process. Why does it matter so much? What is the big deal with a baseball diamond, a triangle, a home metaphor, or some other illustration?

Get Visual

The simple process is more likely to resonate with each person if it is visual. People are more likely to remember it. Consequently, people are more likely to experience the reality of the process if they can recall it.

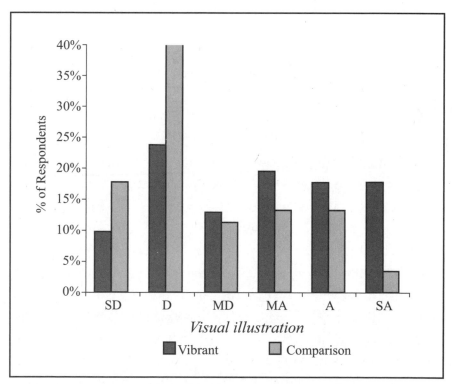

Figure 2. Respondents' level of agreement with having a visual illustration

Note: SD = Strongly disagree; D = Disagree; MD = Moderately disagree;
MA = Moderately agree; A = Agree; SA = Strongly agree

Recollection increases movement. It increases the likelihood that people will progress through the stages of commitment. People will not live out something they cannot remember.

The process must be the vision for discipleship in a local church. The process says, in essence, "This is the kind of people we believe God is calling us to be, and here is *how* He is going to transform us into that type of person." It is personal. It is something each person can internalize and own. The process can become the personal vision for each person in the church.

And vision is always visual.

People are able to live out the vision if they can see it. If there is a visual illustration for the process, people know where they are in the process and where they have yet to go. If they can attach the process to something that is etched in their minds, they are more likely to embrace it.

The process must become etched in the minds of your people.

God is the ultimate etcher. Long before researchers discovered that people remember more when visual stimulation accompanies hearing, God was teaching people visually. He created and crafted people, and He knows what makes them tick. He knows what urges a response in people. The Bible is filled with prophets and teachers who used visual illustrations to stir the hearts of people.

Hosea's life was a poignant visual message for the people. God instructed Hosea to marry an adulteress woman named Gomer (Hosea 1:2). It was probably awkward taking her home to meet his family.

Yet God was making a point.

Gomer was the representation of spiritual adultery committed by God's people. They had forgotten their first love. Each time people looked at the shame of Hosea, they saw a picture of their own relationship with God. When Hosea bought her back, he visually illustrated God's grace in a powerful way.

Jeremiah looked a bit odd stumbling around with an ox yoke on his neck (Jer. 27:2–3). Ox yoke medallions have never been in style and for good reason. However, the image was clear. God was going to discipline His people with a yoke around their necks.

The Passover drama was both bloody and visual. It fore-shadowed the sacrifice of the Lamb of God on the cross. God's implicit instructions on the design of the tabernacle depicted a visual picture of the worship of heaven.

Then there is Jesus. Jesus pointed to fields and birds. He picked up a child and used a fig tree to make a point. He was a visual teacher.

After claiming to be the bread of life, Jesus fed bread to five thousand men (John 6). After calling Himself the light of the world, Jesus put light in a blind man's eyes (John 8–9). After claiming to be the resurrection and the Life, Jesus called Lazarus to come out of the grave (John 11).

The vine and the branches discourse (John 15) most likely involved real vines and branches. The water conversation with the Samaritan woman at the well definitely involved real water (John 4).

If your church is "not into the visual thing," then we assume you do not practice the Lord's Supper (Communion) or bap-tism. Both of these ordinances, given by Christ to the church are visual pictures of a theological reality.

A visual illustration increases clarity; therefore, church leaders should use one. The visual illustration may be a diagram, or it may be a metaphor that gives people a mental picture.

Choose a visual illustration for your process. Get some wise and creative people around a table and come up with one. Or borrow (steal) one from another church. However you do it, just be sure your visual illustration has the following components:

The illustration should be reflective of your process. The illustration must fit. If your process has three steps, then your illustration should reflect that. If your process has four steps, your illustration should reflect that. Ensure that the illustration is an expression of the reality of your process.

The illustration should show progression. Remember the simple process is about moving people toward greater commitment. The genius in the baseball diamond illustration started by Rick Warren is that the diamond shows movement from base to base.

The illustration should help simplify. Don't choose an illustration that makes your process seem complicated. Here is the rule: If you have to explain a lot of symbols and hidden meanings in your illustration, it is too complicated. The point of your visual illustration is to help people grasp the reality.

Define. Illustrate. Measure.

3: Measure

Our research also reveals that measuring your process is critical. Measuring helps bring clarity.

Preseason games are boring to watch, even for serious fans. If you're skimming this chapter while watching a preseason game, it is time to evaluate your life. Perhaps you should get out more. Go ahead, put down the book, and leave the cave.

Seriously, *Sportscenter* on ESPN barely mentions preseason games. The anchors even poke fun at how little the games matter. The best players are not in the game at critical times.

It is basically a practice with real referees. It just seems that no one really cares who wins or loses.

No one cares because the games are not measured.

They do not count. And because the games are not counted in the season's overall record, the games are not taken seriously.

You get the point. For people to take your ministry process seriously, it has to be measured. For people to internalize the simple *how* in your church, you have to evaluate it. The cliché is true: what gets evaluated, gets done.

We asked church leaders if they have a system in place to evaluate if people are progressing through their process.

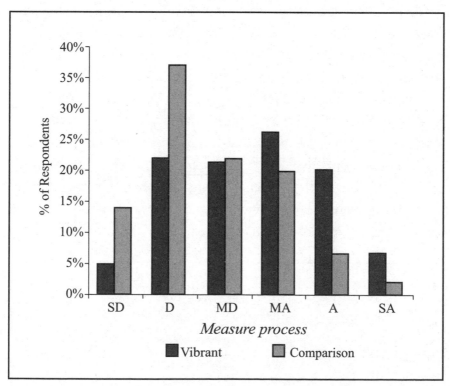

Figure 3. Respondents' level of agreement with measuring the process

Note: SD = Strongly disagree; D = Disagree; MD = Moderately disagree;
MA = Moderately agree; A = Agree; SA = Strongly agree

Church leaders stated their level of agreement with the statement: "We have a system to measure how people progress through the process."

Of the vibrant churches 27 percent strongly agreed or agreed with this compared to 9 percent of the comparison churches. Vibrant church leaders agreed or strongly agreed three times that of the comparison church leaders that they measure the effectiveness of their process. The vast majority of the comparison churches have no system in place to measure people moving through the process (Figure 3).

Michael Hammer, the process expert, indicates that a process must be measured. If there is no measurement, the people within the organization will not internalize the severity and urgency of it.[3] In other words, if you do not measure the process, people will think it does not matter. It will be just another statement on the wall or in the bulletin.

Churches that measure their process prove its value. Measurement proves the process is more than a new fad or down-loadable strategy. Staff, volunteers, and members see the importance.

Measurement also helps leaders know if people are progressing through the process. For example, Cross Church continually evaluates the numbers of people who are moving through their process. Their measurement tool looks like this:

	Love God (worship service)	Love Others (small groups)	Serve World (ministry teams)
Children	120	80	40
Students	140	75	65
Adults	650	400	300
Total	910	555	405

A measurement tool like that at Cross Church focuses on moving people from one level of commitment to another. Holes are easily identified and remedied. If the church increases in attendance at their "love God" level, they expect to increase proportionally at their "love others" and "serve the world" levels.

Are you ready to measure? To measure your process effectively, you must think differently in two critical ways:

Learn to view your numbers horizontally and not vertically. Measuring your process requires you to view your attendance differently from most churches. Take Cross Church's measurement tool, for example. Most church leaders would look at the total number of people in a particular program, such as the total number of adults in small groups. That is looking vertically. It is looking at programs to see if they are successful.

Viewing your numbers horizontally is different. Someone who views numbers horizontally would look at Cross Church and see that a certain percentage of adults moved from a worship service to small groups and then to ministry teams. The horizontal viewer would think of ways to move more people across the chart. Sideways. Horizontally. Got it?

Measure attendance at each level/stage in your process. To evaluate your entire process, you must know how many people are plugged in at each level. Most churches tend to measure only worship attendance and small-group attendance. That makes sense if those are the only two programs in the process. However, it does not make sense if there are additional programs.

For example, Cross Church wants to move people from worship service to small groups to ministry teams. For them to measure effectively, they have to know how many people are in ministry teams. If they did not know that, it would be impossible to see a clear picture of reality.

To get an accurate picture, you must measure attendance at each level. It gives you key knowledge for planning and praying. Without this knowledge, you are bound to make decisions based on incomplete information.

Define it. Illustrate it. Measure it. Discuss it.

4: Discuss

Imagine this scenario. A pastor and team of leaders invest months in crafting a vision or purpose statement. They have late-night meetings with pizza and M&Ms. They debate the wording. They choose key Scriptures to emphasize the direction of the church. They are filled with excitement, and they come up with a plan to share everything with the people.

They share the vision with the key leaders in the church. Then they mail out letters to everyone. They get a banner. They get new letterhead with the statement just under the church name. They even change the names of their budget categories. They put the vision in the bulletin. And the pastor preaches on it for three weeks.

Then everyone breathes a sigh of relief. The intensity dies down. That's it.

"Nice series, Pastor. I enjoyed it."

Everything goes back to normal.

The statement remains, but nothing really changes. It might as well be in a drawer. It is just some nebulous verbiage. No one really pays attention to it. No one really gets it.

This scenario is typical.

If the church is going to be simple, these events cannot happen. The process must not be just another statement on a wall or in a drawer. If the church is going to be simple, the process must be clear.

If the process is going to be clear to the people, then it must get into the very fabric of the church. It must become part of the character of the church. It must be foundational to the church culture. It must be in the DNA of the church's identity.

For the simple process to become woven into the identity of the church, it must be discussed. Frequently. Not just during the launch. Clarity is not realized without consistency.

It is not enough to unveil a vision for the *how* and then bury it among other things. It is insufficient to preach a series on the discipleship process and then file the messages. Consistent discussion is a must.

The Role of Leadership

For the simple process to become a part of the culture of the church, it first must be woven into the leadership culture. The discussion must begin with the leadership of the church. The simple process must become part of their vocabulary. It must roll off their tongues with ease. It must make its way into the hallway discussions, lunches with key leaders, and the meetings.

The process must be discussed among the leaders consistently. If the hearts of the leaders do not beat passionately for it, the people will miss it. If the ministry blueprint is fuzzy to the leaders, it is not even thought about by the people in the church.

Michael Hammer advocates that the leaders of an organization be the pioneers and the overseers of an organization's process. He believes that the leaders of an organization have the breadth of perspective and the authority needed to oversee the entire process and solve problems along the way.[4] He believes that ownership begins with the leaders.

We agree.

Discussion among the leaders leads to understanding and ownership. When the church leadership team discusses the process, the team is able to accept ownership and accountability. They are also able to address problems in the process that hinder the spiritual maturation of the people in the church.

The culture of the church follows the culture of the leadership. The leaders' understanding and ownership overflow to everyone.

According to our research, consistently discussing your ministry process makes a big difference. Simple churches tend to do so while complex churches ignore this principle.

We asked vibrant church leaders and comparison church leaders to evaluate their commitment to discussing the process as a leadership team. We asked both groups of leaders to state their level of agreement with the following statement: "We frequently discuss our process as a leadership team."

Of the vibrant churches, over half of them strongly agreed or agreed with this statement compared to a fourth of the comparison churches. The percentage of vibrant church leaders who agreed or strongly agreed that their church leadership team frequently discusses their process was more than twice that of the comparison church leaders (Figure 4).

The Ongoing Conversation

Our research indicates that you should frequently discuss your simple process. Discussion will lead to understanding and ownership with the leaders. Consequently, the process will be planted deep into the culture of the church.

Perhaps it is time for you to begin the ongoing conversation . . . to get things started.

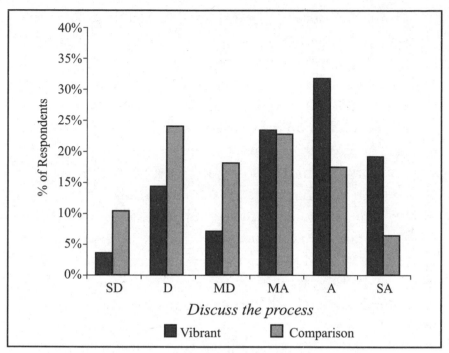

Figure 4. Respondents' level of agreement with discussing the process
Note: SD = Strongly disagree; D = Disagree; MD = Moderately disagree;
MA = Moderately agree; A = Agree; SA = Strongly agree

Pace yourself. This process will take some time. Don't make the mistake of trying to make up for lost time in a few weeks. The discussion must be ongoing. It takes time for understanding and ownership to develop.

Following are four ways to surface and resurface the simple process in discussions among the leadership:

View everything through the lens of your simple process. When you evaluate, evaluate through the lens of your ministry process. When decisions are made, refer to the process. When programs are analyzed, view them through the lens of your ministry process. Bring conversations back to the ministry blueprint.

Surface the process in meetings. The simple process must be discussed in meetings. Sometimes it needs to be an item on the agenda. Other times it just needs to be interwoven into discussions. By using your ministry process language frequently, you will establish a new vocabulary at your church.

Test the leaders on it. No one likes tests, but we took them for years because they provide objective measurement. They actually work. As much as people abhor tests, they hate not passing them even more. It's a bit embarrassing.

Hand out a figure of the visual illustration with fill-in-the-blanks, and have the leaders fill in the answers. Then walk through the visual illustration with the entire group. Don't call people to the front to write in the answers. It is not an algebra class. Simply discuss each part of the process as a group. Let it sink in.

Once a test is given to adults, they will do their best to be prepared for the next one. Make this fun, not serious. Regardless, people will get the point.

Several weeks later, do it again.

Several months later, do it again.

Brainstorm new ways to communicate it. Here is an early warning. Your process will get old. It will lose its freshness. You will one day be tired of the verbiage you chose. At some point the leaders will be sick of talking about it. If you are a type A personality who thrives on change, you may even want to start over.

Ironically, it is just at this point that people in the church are starting to get it.

When the process starts to feel old, brainstorm fresh ways to communicate it. Brainstorm new ways to present your process, and involve other leaders in this. New ideas will keep things fresh and will help you focus on the execution of the process.

Define. Illustrate. Measure. Discuss. All these factors lead to understanding.

5: Increase Understanding

Vibrant churches are confident that people understand their simple ministry process. They have this confidence because they have invested the time in defining, illustrating, measuring, and discussing it.

The comparison churches lack this confidence. They inwardly know that their people do not really understand the ministry blueprint. Often it is because there is no ministry blueprint. Other times, communication has been poor.

We asked the vibrant church leaders and the comparison church leaders to state their level of agreement with the following statement: "Our church members have a clear understanding of our process." Of the vibrant churches, 60 percent agreed at some level with this statement compared to 32 percent of the comparison churches. Moreover, vibrant church leaders agreed or strongly agreed four times that of the comparison church leaders that their church members have a clear understanding of their process (Figure 5).

Understanding does not come easily. It does not occur with a one-time magical act of communication. Increasing understanding is hard work, and it must be continually monitored.

Vibrant church leaders embrace this challenge. They continually and intentionally confirm that their church members have a clear understanding of their process.

And this understanding bears fruit.

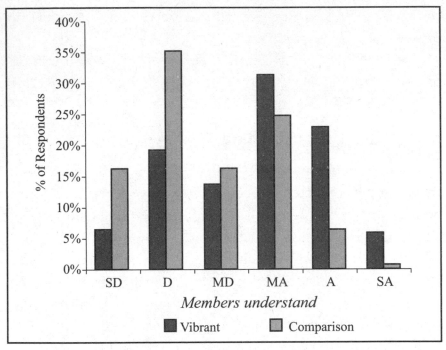

Figure 5. Respondents' level of agreement with members understanding
Note: SD = Strongly disagree; D = Disagree; MD = Moderately disagree;
MA = Moderately agree; A = Agree; SA = Strongly agree

When people understand the process, they are able to embrace it personally. They progress through the process toward spiritual transformation. They partner with the church and God as their spiritual lives are constructed.

When people understand the process, they are also able to bring others through it. People are always the church's greatest resource. And when someone really gets it, the person becomes a missionary and an advocate. The person becomes a walking sermon illustration, a moving and talking billboard for the grace of God. The impact is then exponential.

So, as a leader, you must increase the level of process understanding in your church. To do so, you must do three things. While all three are critical, they are in reverse order of importance:

Articulate the process corporately. Leaders, you must speak about the process to the church as a whole. When you are tired of talking about it, people will just be in the first stages of understanding. That is just the way it works. You are just one voice in their lives.

Max Depree wisely stated, "Leadership is like third grade: it means repeating the significant things."[5] The simple process is significant, and it is worth repeating again and again.

It does not mean you need constantly to devote messages or special days to declaring your ministry process in its entirety. In fact, weaving it into regular messages and communications is more effective because it is consistent.

When you communicate the process, share stories of how it is working. Share stories about how God is moving in the lives of people. Talk about the couple that moved from just coming to church to being the church, to serving others. Talk about the guy who finally tried a small group and is now leading one. Share real stories of real people with real names. It resonates with people, and it leads to understanding.

Share the process interpersonally. More importantly, you must also discuss the process interpersonally with other people. The process must not only be heard through monologue. Dialogue gives people a chance to interact. And this dialogue has a tendency to spread.

Preachers, read this next sentence: It is not enough only to talk about the vision or ministry process from the pulpit. The simple process must be shared at dinner tables and meetings. When people see that it is not just a "sermon thing," it means more. People pay greater attention when they can see your heart off the stage.

Live the process personally. This issue is paramount, the absolutely most important thing you can do to increase understanding. The most important way you help people understand the defined ministry process is through your personal behavior—living and doing what you are asking people to live and do.

If you are asking people to move from a worship service to a small group, you must be in a small group. If you are asking people to progress to a place of service, you must serve in a tangible way . . . off the stage. If you are asking people to connect to people relationally who do not know God, you must meet your neighbors and the person who cuts your hair.

There is another word for it—integrity.

Don't be a spiritual travel agent.

Please, No More Travel Agents

There is a major difference between a travel agent and a tour guide. This difference is seen best in white-water rafting. There are plenty of rafting outfitters from which to choose along a white-water river trail. A travel agent will mail you brochures. A travel agent will suggest a few rafting outfitters and a river to enjoy.

But a travel agent's role ends there.

A travel agent spouts out intellectual information, hands you some brochures, and smiles. A travel agent tells you to enjoy the journey.

"Nice to meet you. Enjoy the trip."

A tour guide is different.

Along the Ocoee, in the Smoky Mountains, there is a great tour guide named Tripp. The name fits. He literally is a trip.

Unlike the travel agent who hands you a brochure, he goes *with* you on the journey.

"Nice to meet you. Get in. Let's go."

Tripp knows the Ocoee. He knows each rapid intimately and talks about them with great energy. Double Suck. Moonshot. Flipper. Tripp enjoys each stage in the journey. It is fun to hear him share stories about the different parts of the river. You fall more in love with the river and the scenery because of him. You are inspired by his passion.

What makes Tripp a great tour guide is not his information. Even some of the local travel agents have the information. Tripp is great because of his love for the journey and because he takes you with him.

He takes you along the journey he has traveled. He does not instruct from a distance. He is with you. He is on the bus with you from the outfitter to the river. He is in the raft with you. And, if things do not go as planned, he is in the river with you.

Tripp has been where he is taking you. He is able to instruct because he is familiar with the journey. He speaks from a place of personal authority, and you listen. He is not perfect. His boat may tip over with you in it. But he is credible.

People need spiritual tour guides. They have had plenty of spiritual travel agents. Be a tour guide through the process of spiritual transformation in your church. Take people on a journey with you.

If you get in the boat, the ministry process will come alive. The ministry blueprint will make sense then. It will be clear.

Clarity is a huge first step, but it is only the beginning. You must now proceed to movement, the removal of congestion in your church.

We think you will have fun in the next stage, but be careful. You may start messing with sacred cows. Please seek God's wisdom for the right pace of change.

Let's see how you do in the chapter.

GROUP DISCUSSION QUESTIONS

1. According to our weekly programs, what kind of disciples are we trying to make?
2. Is there a defined process at our church? If so, what is it? How is each of our weekly programs used?
3. What is the illustration or metaphor we most often use to describe spiritual growth?
4. How do we measure success at our church? What are we looking for?
5. On a scale of one to ten (with ten being the highest), what is the level of process understanding in our church?
6. What should we do in response to the things learned in this chapter?
7. Are we tour guides or travel agents?

SIX

Movement:
Removing Congestion

*And we, who with unveiling faces, all reflect the
Lord's glory, are being transformed into his likeness
with ever-increasing glory, which comes from
the Lord, who is the Spirit.*
~ THE APOSTLE PAUL, 2 CORINTHIANS 3:18 NIV

Clarity ➤➤ Movement ➤➤ Alignment➤➤ Focus

Congestion is very frustrating.

It does not take empirical research to validate the casual observation that people hate rush-hour traffic. You can see it on their faces. You can see it on the gripped steering wheels. You can see it by the certain hand motions offered to other drivers.

Congestion during rush hour is painful. The flow of traffic is stopped. People creep along at a snail's pace. The roads were not designed to handle that many people at one time. There is nowhere for all the cars to go. So everyone sits and waits.

Head or chest congestion is also a nuisance. You can see it on the somber faces of those struggling to breathe. When you have congestion, your day seems longer than normal. Your head or chest hurts. You don't feel like talking because you sound funny.

Congestion in the head or chest prevents movement. The movement of air is hampered because of congestion. Your head or chest is full of stuff that is not supposed to be there. Mucus, phlegm, and junk clog your body. The extra stuff prevents your sinuses from functioning properly.

Congestion stinks.

Many churches are congested.

Spiritual movement is stifled. The building of lives is slowed. And these congested churches are filled with the same people. We are not referring to the absence of new people, although that is telling as well. We are referring to people staying the same. Unchanged. Unmoved.

We are talking about people not being transformed. Week after week, year after year, many people are the same. The building project of people's lives is stalled. Stagnant believers and congested churches go hand in hand.

Sadly, in many churches people are stuck in the same place spiritually. And there is no intentional process to move them.

The Bible paints a different picture of spiritual growth. According to Scripture a believer's life is to be transformed more and more. People are not supposed to be the same. There is to be progression, movement.

Our churches should be filled with people who are becoming. Becoming more like Christ. Becoming more loving and joyful. Becoming. Being transformed.

Unveiled Faces

Second Corinthians 3:18 says, "And we, who with unveiled faces all reflect the Lord's glory, are being transformed into his likeness with ever-increasing glory, which comes from the Lord, who is the Spirit" (NIV).

Paul is taking the readers back to Moses. Moses would walk up to this mountain called Mount Sinai. There he would meet with God face-to-face. It was the place where God gave Moses the Ten Commandments. Each time Moses went to meet with God on this mountain, he came back glowing.

He had an encounter with God on Mount Sinai, and this encounter was so remarkable that Moses was transformed. His appearance was altered. He shone. He looked different. The first time he came down from the mountain, people were even afraid. The change was that significant.

Moses would wear a veil over his face when he came down from the mountain. He wore a veil to cover the fading glory (2 Cor. 3:13). Once Moses left the presence of God, the glory would fade. With each step away from the mountain, the glory would decrease.

Moses had a veiled face. We have *unveiled* faces.

We do not have to wear a veil because the glory is not diminishing. In fact the opposite is true. The glory is ever *increasing*. It is so because we never leave the presence of God. We never come back down the mountain.

The mountain is in us.

His Spirit lives within us. We have a relationship with God that even Moses did not have. We are in the new covenant that brings righteousness, not the old covenant that brings death (2 Cor. 3:9). Moses had to go to the mountain to behold the glory of God. We don't. We have a greater level of intimacy.

Just as God transformed Moses, He transforms us when we place ourselves in His presence. The word for *transform* is in the passive voice and present tense. The passive voice indicates that we do not transform ourselves. God is the one who does the transforming.

The present tense indicates that this transforming is currently taking place. Right now. As you read this. Transformation is not only a past event. God is also about right now.

The word from transformation is *metamorphosis*. It means to change the essential nature of something. It is a real change, not just a change on the outside. The core of something is changed. The word is used to describe the process a caterpillar goes through to become a butterfly. The nasty, wormy, creepy, crawly insect becomes a beautiful butterfly. The process is metamorphosis.

God desires to bring His people through this morphing process. He seeks to transform the people in Your church into His image. And He wants to do so with ever-increasing glory. Meaning He wants the people you serve to be more like Him tomorrow than they are today.

Congested churches and stagnant believers are the antithesis of God's plan.

Since God is the one who transforms the people in your church, what is your part?

Your Part

What did Moses do to be transformed? What was his part?

Think about it. God did the transforming, but Moses played a vital role in the process. What was his part? What is your part?

Moses walked up the mountain. Moses placed himself in the right place to be transformed by God. He discovered the place where God would move in his life, and he put himself there.

Church leaders must do the same. Your part as a church leader is to place people in the pathway of God's transforming power. Your part is to design a process that partners with the transformation process revealed in Scripture.

Simple church leaders have done just this. They have designed a ministry process that puts people in the place for God to transform them. The ministry process is not where the power lies. Only God does the transforming.

However, God has designed spiritual growth to be a process. It is to occur with ever-increasing glory. And simple church leaders have chosen to partner with God in this process.

Simple church leaders have designed their simple process with movement in mind. The ministry process moves people to greater levels of commitment—with ever-increasing levels of discipleship. The simple process moves people through the process of spiritual transformation.

Congestion is gone.

Movement occurs naturally. People are not stuck in the same place. There is a plan for transformation. People are challenged to progress through the simple process. Change in the lives of people is expected.

According to our research, there is a significant relationship between the vitality of a local church and the movement of the church's ministry process. Movement is *the sequential steps in the process that causes people to move to greater areas of commitment*.

Do you have a simple process that moves people? Or is your church body full of congestion?

Thankfully for the sake of your head or chest, there is medicine designed to unclog your sinuses. There is medication prescribed to bring the movement of air back to your sinus system. Likewise in this chapter you will be given five prescriptions to unclog your process, to remove the congestion.

All five prescriptions are essential and have been validated by our research.

If you want your process to move people, your programming must be strategic and sequential. You must also intentionally move people, offer a clear next step, and provide a class for new members.

1. Strategic Programming

According to our research, strategic programming is extremely important.

We asked vibrant and comparison church leaders if they have intentionally placed programs to work in conjunction with their ministry process. We asked them to state their level of agreement with the following statement: "We have placed our programs along our strategic process" (Figure 1).

Of the vibrant churches, 54 percent strongly agreed or agreed with the statement compared to 30 percent of the comparison churches. The vibrant churches were much more likely to place their weekly programs along their simple process.

Simple church leaders are strategic with their programming. They abhor the concept of doing programs because of tradition or the need to have something on the calendar. They view programs as tools to place people in the pathway of God's morphing.

Northpoint Community Church has strategically placed steps along their simple process. They began with their process and placed appropriate steps/programs accordingly. Each

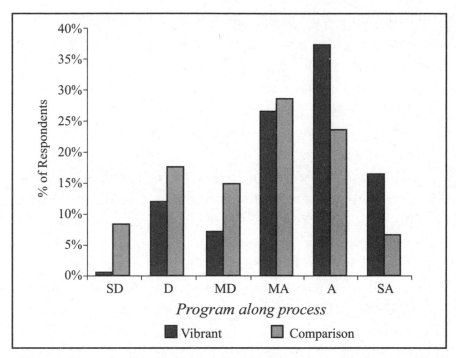

Figure 1. Respondents' level of agreement with item programming along process

Note: SD = Strongly disagree; D = Disagree; MD = Moderately disagree;
MA = Moderately agree; A = Agree; SA = Strongly agree

program is designed to move people from the foyer to the kitchen. Several lessons on how to program strategically can be learned from Northpoint and other simple churches. Following are a few of the lessons we have observed.

Begin with your clearly defined process. Placing your programs along your process is an extension of the clarity element. It is matching your programs with the simple process God has given your church.

However, you must begin with the process, not the programs. If you begin with the programs, you will have a tendency to build a process around the programs. If the programs do not fit into your process, you need to eliminate them. You will find more on this issue in chapter 8.

Choose one program for each phase of your process. For each department in your church, there should be one program for each phase of your process. The temptation is to attach all of your existing programs to one aspect of your process. While the intentions are good, doing so will not simplify your ministry. Multiple programs for each phase of the process divide attention and energy.

Design each program for a specific aspect of the process. After you have chosen one program for each phase of the process, be sure that program effectively engages people in that aspect of the process.

Each program should be distinct from the others. The program fulfills a different phase of the process and must have a unique identity. Do not let other priorities clutter the purpose of the program. Protect it. Each program is a critical part of the overall picture. Be sure that program is done with excellence. Constantly evaluate it. Constantly tweak it.

Place the programs in sequential order. Speaking of movement, we are now at a perfect place to move to the next prescription: sequential programming.

2. Sequential Programming

Programs must be placed along your ministry process, and they also must be placed in sequential order. According to our research, sequential programming is vital.

We asked vibrant and comparison church leaders if their programs are offered in sequence. We asked them to state their level of agreement with the following statement: "Our programs are sequential, based on our process" (Figure 2).

Of the vibrant churches, 37 percent strongly agreed or agreed with this statement compared to 15 percent of the

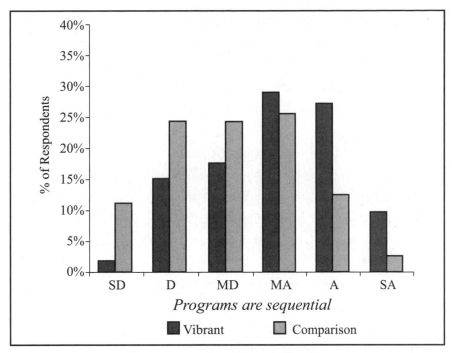

Figure 2. Respondents' level of agreement with sequential programming
Note: SD = Strongly disagree; D = Disagree; MD = Moderately disagree;
MA = Moderately agree; A = Agree; SA = Strongly agree

comparison churches. The vibrant churches are more than twice as likely as the comparison churches to set up their programs sequentially.

Back to Rafting

Let's go back to the Ocoee. You know, the river where Tripp is our tour guide.

The white-water rafting trip on the Ocoee follows a simple process. The designers of the rafting expedition sequentially designed the experience. There is wisdom in the sequential ordering of the rafting journey.

For example, the journey begins on a slower part of the river. The designers don't throw you in at an advanced level. They place the rafts in the river at a location where you will experience greater rapids the longer you are on the river. You begin with a level one rapid and work your way up, with ever-increasing glory.

The photographer is even placed at a strategic place along the journey. Your picture is taken as you are battling the strongest rapid of the day. You can bring home an enlarged photograph to show your friends how brave you are.

Here is how the sequential process of the rafting experience unfolds:

First, you get connected to the concept of rafting. The experience does not begin with a jump in the river. The trip does not begin with taking on a level four rapid. It begins with an orientation, selection of the appropriate gear, and meeting your tour guide. You put on the gear and board the bus. You see the river and hear stories about it. You are now along for the ride. You have agreed to go on the journey.

Second, you get to know the people in your raft. You share stories with other people in your raft. You need each person. You could not paddle the river alone. The tour guide stresses that safety depends on teamwork. And the people make the journey exciting. Part of the experience is hearing the shouts from the people in your boat.

Third, you become a contributor. At first, the tour guide does most of the work. However, as the journey progresses, the rapids get stronger. And he needs everyone in the boat to paddle. You get to help. Your two strokes forward or three stokes backward make a difference.

You go home telling the story. You call families and friends from your cell phone, once you are back in service range.

Which, if you have a certain cellular company, may not happen for a long time. Regardless, you have pictures and memories, and you desire to bring others with you on the journey.

If the rafting journey were not designed with sequence, it would be a horrible experience. Imagine if you were tossed to a level four rapid without knowing the people in your boat or without having your gear. Imagine being placed in the middle of the river without knowing your tour guide or how to row.

Without proper sequence the experience would not be meaningful to you. It would be a miserable day. You might even bail out before the journey is complete. You would not develop a love for white-water rafting or the people in the boat. You would leave with no desire to bring others through the experience you endured.

The designers of the experience strategically place the events of the day to happen in logical sequence. By doing so, they enable rafters to progress through the day with joy. Rafters are able to move through the journey with confidence because they are prepared for each upcoming challenge.

Sequence produces movement.

Likewise, sequential programming produces movement.

Simple church leaders have learned the wisdom of sequential programming. By placing the programs in sequence along the process, the programs truly become tools to facilitate the process of transformation. Congestion is conquered. People move through the process simply by moving to the next level of programming.

As you sequentially place programs along your ministry process, here are three essentials to guide your thinking.

Order the sequence of your programs to reflect your process. In other words, the order of the programming must flow from the order of the process. For example, the order of Cross Church's process is love God, love others, and serve the world. The sequence of their programming reflects this process.

The first program in Cross Church's sequence is their weekend worship services (love God). The next level of programming at Cross Church is their small-group program (love others). The final level of programming is their ministry team structure (serve the world).

At Cross Church, it would be confusing if the first program in the sequential process were their small-group program. It would not match their stated process. Their stated process begins with "love God." The program they have matched with that aspect of their process is their weekend services. Therefore, the first program in their sequence must be the weekend worship services.

This issue is not a small detail. The sequence matters because you want people to move through the simple ministry process. If you place the programs sequentially, people will move through your process simply by moving from one program to the next. As people are progressing through the programming, they will be simultaneously moving through the process that God has given your church.

Designate a clear entry-point to your process. The entry-point is the first level of programming in your simple process. Without a clear entry point, there is no beginning to the process. When a process lacks a clear beginning, it is definitely not simple.

The entry point is the program through which people are most likely to enter your church. It is the weekly program that guests are most likely to attend. It is the program you encourage your people to invite friends to attend.

Once you have designated a clear entry point to your process, treat your program that way. Do it with excellence. Know that new people will form an impression of God and your church based on what they see and hear.

Identify the next levels of programming. Just as you have designated an entry point, identify the next levels of programming in your process. What program do you desire people to attend after they have been to your entry-point program? What is the program you want them to attend after that?

The commitment should increase with each level of programming. Therefore, attendance at the subsequent levels of programming will decrease as commitment increases. That is not a bad thing. It is clarifying the levels of commitment in your church. Everyone is at different places in the journey. Each person is a work in progress.

Once you have placed your programs strategically and sequentially along your process, the real challenge begins. Strategic and sequential programming is vital, but that can all be done on paper. It does not involve real people. The challenge is moving people through the process. The challenge is making it happen. This is the essence of intentional movement.

3. Intentional Movement

Johnny Lechner is finally moving on. Actually the University of Wisconsin at Whitewater is forcing him to graduate. He has been there too long. He is targeted to receive his diploma in May. You probably know someone who squeezed a four-year degree into five or six years, but he has gone well beyond that.

Lechner has been in college for twelve years.

That's right—twelve years. He is almost thirty. This entire time he has been working on his bachelor's degree. He has been allowed to be in matriculation purgatory for three times the length of an average collegian.

Lechner still dresses like a college student or poster child from Abercrombie and Fitch. He still goes to college parties. In fact, one of his major goals for his final year was to go on two spring break trips. He is such an overachiever. He even ran for a position on student government with the platform of his collegiate experience.

On late-night talk shows, Lechner says that he likes college. Just in case you were unsure. He enjoys the carefree lifestyle and the avoidance of real-world responsibilities. He likes sleeping late, playing some music, going to a couple of classes, and then hanging out with friends. Staying in the same place is comfortable for him. College has become a perpetual comfort zone for Lechner.

While many think his situation is ridiculous, are not many churches structured the same way? In these churches, people remain in the same place spiritually for years. And sometimes they remain in the same groups. They are kept in some type of spiritual holding tank. They rarely move to greater levels of commitment.

They are in a perpetual comfort zone.

Simple churches fight the Lechner syndrome. They resist congestion. They intentionally move people from program to program through their ministry process.

According to our research, intentionally moving people through your ministry process is vital. We asked vibrant and comparison churches if they use their programming to do so. We asked them to state their level of agreement with the following statement: "We are intentional about moving people from one program to another" (Figure 3).

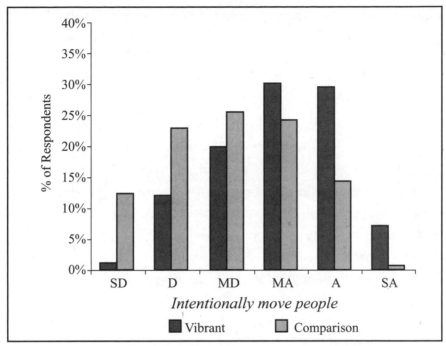

Figure 3. Respondents' level of agreement with intentional movement

Note: SD = Strongly disagree; D = Disagree; MD = Moderately disagree;
MA = Moderately agree; A = Agree; SA = Strongly agree

Of the vibrant churches, 37 percent strongly agreed or agreed with this statement compared to 15 percent of the comparison churches. Vibrant churches are more than twice as likely as comparison churches to move people from program to program.

Remember, simple church leaders are designers. They design opportunities for people to be transformed. Complex church leaders are programmers. Programmers focus on one program at a time. Designers focus on the movement between the programs.

Without movement, programs are an end to themselves. Without movement you are just running ministry programs.

To maximize movement in your church, consider the following four suggestions.

Create Short-term Steps

As you seek to move people from one program to another, think in terms of short-term steps. How can you help people make steps toward the next program in your process?

The steps should not be new programs. They should be short-term opportunities that expose people to an aspect of the process that they have not yet experienced.

Saddleback Church has been a pioneer of short-term steps. The process at Saddleback seeks to move people from worship services to small groups. To help people make that step, Saddleback occasionally offers short-term groups that are promoted in conjunction with the worship services.

Saddleback, led by Rick Warren, was the first church to launch forty-day spiritual growth campaigns. During these campaigns Saddleback aligns all of the teaching in the church around the same theme. For six weeks the small groups engage curriculum that relates to the messages delivered in the worship services.

All of the people are then challenged to join a small group for just six weeks. It is a short-term step. People who have not yet moved to a small group are receptive to this six-week challenge. They know that their commitment has a predetermined amount of time to it; therefore, they are more willing to give it a try.

While they receive the content of the series, they also move farther along in the spiritual transformation process. Many of the groups continue to meet after the series is finished.

At Christ Fellowship in Miami (Eric's church), the process is designed to move people from worship service to small groups and then to ministry. To help move people from the small group to the ministry aspect of the process, all groups were recently challenged to serve together beyond the walls of the church. It was a short-term challenge. Groups participated in one serving-beyond opportunity over a two-month period. Many people were exposed for the first time to the serving part of the process.

Capitalize on Relationships

People do not progress through the simple process because they hear it from the pulpit. People do not move through the process because they see a purpose statement on the wall. As helpful as these things can be, people move because someone else brings them through the process.

Relationships bridge the process.

Since relationships are so vital, set up relational connections between the programs. Remember, it is the handoffs that count. Movement is what happens in between the programs. Movement is *how* someone is *handed off* from one program to another.

Here is an example. Linda is a thirty-two-year-old mom who is attending worship services. Her husband only comes with her occasionally. She is a believer and recently has sensed a hunger to grow deeper in her faith. While she attends fairly regularly, she does not have deep relationships at the church. The people she does know well are only as involved as she is. Or less.

She has heard that there is a small group for young mothers at her church. Her church desires to move people from worship services to small groups. They are designing these groups with people like Linda in mind.

Here are two approaches to getting her into a small group.

Approach 1: The church puts a list of small groups in the worship folder. Linda hears a challenge from the stage to come to one of these groups. The times are listed along with the rooms or homes where the groups are located. She knows no one at the group. She is not even sure where the street is located. She is afraid if she does not like it, she will feel awkward or guilty not returning.

Approach 2: The church puts the same list in the worship folder, but they do more. They have a small-group registration booth where leaders of the groups meet people and answer questions. Linda can go to the registration booth and meet the leader of the young mother's group. While she is at the booth, she meets other women who are inquiring about the group. The relationships alleviate her fears.

The second approach contains a small difference that makes a big impact. The difference is relational. Relationships, not information, bridge the process. Capitalize on the power of relationships.

Consider the "Now What?"

No matter where a person is, God is seeking to bring him or her farther on the spiritual journey. Christ meets people where they are, but He keeps pulling them farther along. Transformation is His work. And He is never finished.

Your programming should be an expression of how you believe God works in the lives of people. As you are seeking to move people through your process, always consider the "now what?" Do not let the present program be the end. Seek to move people farther along.

Practically, it means encouraging people at the present level of programming to move to the next level. View the present program as a bridge to the next program in the process.

During our consultation at Cross Church, we noticed the senior pastor referred to his small group during his sermon. The message was clear: "This worship service is not the end. There is something else for you. And for me." It was not a point in his message. The comment was simply woven into the fabric of his message. And his church. At the conclusion of the service, announcements were made regarding small groups. Cross Church nailed the "now what?".

Connect People to Groups

Groups are set up differently, and they have a variety of names: Sunday school, small groups, Bible fellowship classes, community groups, ministry teams, cell groups, home groups, and bowling leagues. OK, we are joking about the bowling league. But you get the point. Groups are offered in a variety of ways.

While the purpose and style of each group varies, they all connect people relationally. As you are seeking to move people, move them to some type of group.

Thom's previous research on effective churches is convincing. What he said several years ago still rings true: "The picture is clear: people stick to a church when they get involved in a small group."[1]

If people only come to a service, they can drop out without anyone knowing. When people move to a group, they are known. They are able to live life with other people. They enjoy the ride with other people in the raft.

When people move to a group, they stick. They stay. They last. They have a support network, a community of fellow Christ followers. They continue in the life of the church. They are still being transformed.

Strategic programming, sequential programming, and intentional movement are essential prescriptions for removing congestion in the body of Christ. They are broad and are directly related to the programming involved in a simple process. The next two prescriptions are specific steps that reveal a church's commitment to movement.

4. Clear Next Step

Stories of orphans in countries like Romania and Russia have grabbed the hearts of many Americans. Children are placed in large orphanages with hundreds of other children. The number of caretakers in each orphanage is extremely low. The ratio of adults to children is shocking.

All the caretaker can do is be sure each child has his or her basic needs met. Food, water, shelter. However, the children are not touched. They are not hugged. They are not nurtured.

A decade ago journalists first entered these orphanages. They were shocked at what they did not see or hear. There was no laughter. No tears. Three-year-olds could not speak or cry.

Without touch the orphanages were void of laughter and tears. Without touch the children's growth was stunted. Without nurture, they did not mature normally. The lack of attention was damaging to the children.

Unfortunately, many churches treat new believers like these orphanages treat children. There is little attention and nurture.

New believers are tossed aside. There is typically no follow-up. The person is unsure what to do next.

This situation is tragic. Just as children need nurture and attention during their formative years, so do new believers. There must be a clear next step for them. They must be moved into the life of the church. They must be nurtured toward spiritual growth.

According to our research, offering a clear next step for new believers is essential. We asked vibrant and comparison church leaders about their treatment of new believers. We asked them to state their level of agreement with the following statement: "After someone becomes a believer, the next step for them in the spiritual transformation process is clear."

Of the vibrant churches, 48 percent strongly agreed or agreed with this statement compared to 22 percent of the non-growing churches. The vibrant churches are more than twice as likely as the comparison churches to offer a clear next step to new believers (Figure 4).

It makes sense that vibrant churches are more careful in their treatment of new believers than comparison churches. New believers are often the most vocal missionaries a church has. They still know lost people. They have a fire in them that many older believers lose. New believers have not learned all the religious rules yet. They talk freely about the grace they have discovered.

New believers are the greatest resource your church has to influence the community. When vibrant churches nurture new believers, they are nurturing the movement of the gospel.

While nurturing new believers produces fruit, it is also the right thing to do, whether it produces any result or not. These new believers are real people. They are not just names on a list. They have real lives, jobs, and families. They have just crossed

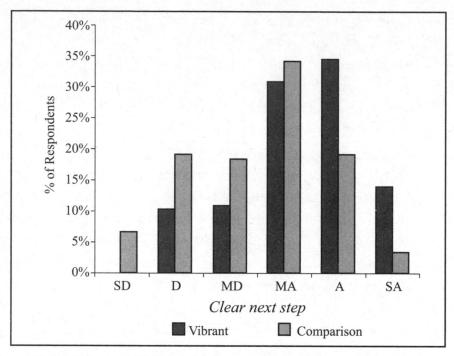

Figure 4. Respondents' level of agreement with providing a clear next step
Note: SD = Strongly disagree; D = Disagree; MD = Moderately disagree;
MA = Moderately agree; A = Agree; SA = Strongly agree

the line of faith into a new world. They are as new to this world as a baby is to his new surroundings. They need someone to walk with them in this new world. They need a clear next step.

A Look at the Next Step

Many of the simple and vibrant churches we researched use some type of group for new believers. They either provide a group for new believers, or they match individuals up with an existing group. Regardless of the approach, plugging new believers into a group is effective. Thom discovered in a previous study that "new Christians who immediately became active in a small group are five times more likely to remain in the church five years later than those who were active in worship services alone."[2]

Other simple churches we researched provided new believers with a personal mentor or discipleship leader. The two people meet for several weeks in an informal setting to go through some type of curriculum. Or the mentor simply helps the new Christian get plugged into the life of the church.

Whatever your strategy is with new believers, have a strategy! Discipleship of new believers does not just happen. It must be intentional. There must be a heartbeat and a plan to make it happen.

Simple churches move new believers into the life of the church. They also are purposeful in their treatment of new members.

5. New Members Class

There is an orientation for almost everything these days. If you move into a new neighborhood that has a homeowners association, you will probably be invited to a new residents meeting. If your child heads to college this fall, you will send him or her to a new student orientation—not covered in the tuition. For new drivers there is a class.

Eric recently thought about exchanging his reading glasses for contacts. Then he was told he would need to attend an orientation on how to "install" them properly. He is still using the glasses. Who has time for a class on contact lenses? Eric's doctor will not allow him to get contacts. His commitment is too low.

There is an orientation for almost everything these days. Except for joining many churches.

It seems that the commitment to buy contact lenses is greater than the commitment to join many churches. Most churches only require new members to fill out a card or a triplicate form. It happens so fast. Expectations are minimal. Signing up for a department store credit card takes more time.

Simple churches, however, tend to require new members classes.

According to our research, it is critical that you use some type of new member training to move new people effectively into the life of the church. We asked vibrant and comparison church leaders to state their level of agreement with the following statement: "We have a class or group to move new people into the life of the church" (Figure 5).

Of the vibrant churches, 70 percent strongly agreed or agreed with this statement compared to 38 percent of the comparison churches. The vibrant churches are much more likely than the comparison churches to offer a new members class.

Thom has commented numerous times on the importance of a new members class. After studying churches that effectively reach the unchurched, he stated, "The relationship between assimilation effectiveness and a new members class is amazing. Churches that require potential members to attend a new members class have a much higher retention rate than those who do not."[3]

The impact is amazing. So we are not surprised that vibrant churches use new members classes to move people into the life of the church. It just confirms what has already been established.

However, we are surprised that so many churches still do not offer any type of new member training. The evidence is and has been compelling. Offer a class for new members!

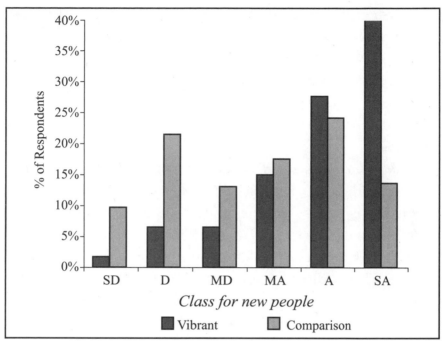

Figure 5. Respondents' level of agreement with new members class

Note: SD = Strongly disagree; D = Disagree; MD = Moderately disagree;
MA = Moderately agree; A = Agree; SA = Strongly agree

Typically at new members groups or classes, the beliefs, practices, and direction of the church are discussed. People get a chance to understand exactly what they are joining. They hear the heartbeat of your church. Great dialogue occurs, and people walk away with a deeper connection to your church.

In addition, we have observed that simple church leaders use their new member training to teach their process and ask for commitment. We encourage you to include both of these in your new member orientation.

Teach the simple process. People enter churches with various kinds of backgrounds and experiences. Some people join with a preconceived idea of how a church should operate. Some even come with strong feelings about programs they believe the church should offer.

The new members class can serve as a filter for ministry philosophy at your church. It is a great opportunity to teach the simple process that God has given your church. People are given an opportunity to know up front *how* your church functions.

Ask for commitment to the process. The new member training is the only time church leaders have exclusively with potential members. Simple church leaders maximize this time by asking for commitment. They clearly define how a member can progress through the process of spiritual transformation. They indicate that moving through the process is the expectation.

Your new member training is the opportunity to invite new people to join you on the journey. Use the time wisely. Ask for commitment. Challenge your potential members to bring others through the ministry process.

Back to Jesus

If anyone knows discipleship, it is Jesus.

His method of discipleship was simple.

Jesus drew twelve men to Himself, trained them, and unleashed the movement of the gospel through them. In fact, you are reading this today because these men got serious about their calling. Jesus had no plan B. The disciples were the plan. He left the message in their hands.

Most people would have done it differently. Most people would have chosen another method to be sure people heard about his sacrifice. He did have every resource available to Him. After all, He is God.

He could have chosen to broadcast His death and resurrection to the entire world. He could have preached it loudly from the heavens. He could have had angels disperse gospel tracts from the cosmos.

Instead He simply poured Himself into His disciples.

Encountering Jesus and His disciples in the gospels provides a snapshot of a simple discipleship process. In the Gospel of Luke, three distinct phases emerge: calling, building, and sending. These three phases are sequential and are designed to move the disciples toward greater levels of commitment.

The Calling (Luke 5–6)

In Luke 5, Jesus calls the disciples to Himself. Jesus provided them with opportunities to encounter and experience Him. He interacted with them relationally and on their turf. He went fishing with Peter, James, and John. He went to a party at Matthew's house. And He asked each of them to follow Him.

In Luke 6, Jesus cemented their calling. After spending the night praying, He appointed twelve guys to be His apostles. They were now going to be recognized as His disciples, as belonging to Him.

The Building (Luke 7–8)

After calling the disciples to Himself, He provided them with opportunities designed to build their faith. In Luke 7, He exposed them to critical teaching. They learned about having an eternal view, rejoicing, loving enemies, not judging others, and bearing spiritual fruit.

In Luke 8, He allowed them to observe Him on the front lines of ministry. They saw Him heal people and raise the dead.

They saw Him calm a storm. They also learned how to treat people by watching Jesus. They saw His love and compassion toward people who society shunned. He defended the worship of a repentant, sinful woman, and He referred to another woman as daughter.

The Sending (Luke 9)

After the calling and building phases, Jesus now turned ministry over to His disciples. He provided them opportunities to grow by serving. In Luke 9, Jesus sent out His disciples to do ministry together. They came back for debriefing. Perhaps Jesus sat around the campfire with His disciples and listened intently to their stories. It was a great teaching moment. Serving always is.

Later in Luke 9, Jesus invited the disciples to participate in the feeding of the five thousand. He said to them, "You give them something to eat." They passed out the baskets and participated in the miracle.

While Jesus sent them to do ministry, He still provided instruction and encouragement. Jesus rescued them from a ministry opportunity that did not quite go as planned. The disciples had tried to cast a demon out of a boy but could not. It was probably rather embarrassing. The father came to Jesus begging for help. Jesus stepped in and brought healing. Jesus intentionally placed them in a position to be spiritually stretched.

Jesus called, built, and sent His disciples. He strategically and sequentially placed them in a position to move to greater levels of commitment and growth.

His discipleship process was simple. It was not stagnant or congested.

It had movement.

Take the prescriptions. Be sure your church removes the congestion. Then your church will be ready to get everyone on the same page. We call that alignment, the subject of the next chapter.

GROUP DISCUSSION QUESTIONS

1. What has been our view of spiritual growth? Does it match 2 Corinthians 3:13?
2. Is our church congested? Where?
3. Are our programs placed along a process?
4. What is the sequence of our programming?
5. Do we have a clear step for new believers?
6. What should we do about our new members class or lack of one?

SEVEN

Alignment: Maximizing the Energy of Everyone

Now I urge you, brothers, in the name of our Lord Jesus Christ, that you all say the same thing, that there be no divisions among you, and that you be united with the same understanding and the same conviction.
~ THE APOSTLE PAUL, 1 CORINTHIANS 1:10

Clarity ➻ Movement ➻ Alignment ➻ Focus

Do you believe in miracles? Yes!"

That is perhaps the most famous call in sports broadcasting history. Announcer Al Michaels yelled it as the United States' hockey team pulled off one of the greatest upsets of all time. Their epic defeat of the Soviet hockey team is referred to as "the miracle on ice."

The movie *Miracle* tells the story of the 1980 United States Olympic hockey team that shocked the world. Two days after beating the Russians, the U.S. team defeated Finland and won the gold medal.

Why was it considered a miracle?

The Soviet team had held the gold medal for the previous twenty years. They were by far the most dominant hockey team in the world. They had recently destroyed an all-star team of professional players from the National Hockey League. The U.S. Olympic team was all amateurs, mostly college kids. They were seeded twelve in the tournament. No one but themselves believed they could win.

Herb Brooks was charged with assembling and coaching the group of amateurs. Before the dream of gold could become a reality, he had to align the team around the same approach to hockey. He had to maximize everyone's energy.

It was a daunting task. The guys came from different backgrounds, colleges, and parts of the country. They came with their own approaches and styles of play.

Unity did not come easily. They were a group of individuals, not a team aligned on the same agenda. Each player identified with his former team, not the Olympic team. *Miracle* depicts Brooks during practices asking players, "Who do you play for?". Each player responds with the name of his college team.

Brooks knew this had to change.

After a halfhearted performance in an exhibition game, Coach Brooks decided it was time to push for alignment. After the guys had played an entire game, he had them skate. This is the hockey equivalent of a football team running laps or a basketball team doing suicide runs.

It was a defining moment for the team.

During the brutal workout, one of the players yelled out, "I play for the United States of America." With that statement Brooks dismissed the players. It was the turning point. The group of individuals became one. They no longer saw themselves as playing for different schools but as playing for the United States of America.

They became a team. Each player became a part of the greater whole. Each player committed to align himself to the team's approach to hockey. The energy and contribution of each individual was maximized. It was beautiful. And the impact was great.

The Miracle of Unity

Do you believe in miracles?

Through the sacrificial death of Christ, believers are one with God. Theologians call it the atonement. It is the miracle of salvation. A holy God and sinful man unified.

God also desires the miracle of unity for the church—for your church. Much more is at stake than an Olympic gold medal. Lives hang in the balance. Without the miracle of unity, churches divide and ministry suffers. And all this occurs while the world watches.

In the finality of Jesus' life, He was burdened for unity. In the garden He prayed that believers would be one. He said to the Father, "May they all be one, as You, Father, are in Me and I am in You. May they also be one in Us, so the world may believe You sent Me" (John 17:21).

That is a huge statement.

Jesus prayed that His followers would be as unified as He and the Father are. God the Father, the Son, and the Holy Spirit are completely one. They are inseparable. Jesus prayed that believers would be that intimate, that united, that aligned. Unity reflects the glory and character of God because God is unified.

Jesus continued, "I have given them the glory You have given Me. May they be one as We are one. I am in them and You are in Me. May they be made completely one, so the world may know You have sent Me and have loved them as You have loved Me" (John 17:22–23).

Not only does unity reflect God's character, but it also gets the attention of the world. People are attracted to unity. Jesus said earlier that all people would know we are His disciples by the love that we have for one another" (John 13:35).

The apostle Paul encouraged the same. He challenged the church to be "thinking the same way, having the same love, sharing the same feelings, focusing on one goal" (Phil. 2:2).

Unity is powerful. It is magnetic. It is a beautiful thing. And the impact is great. Such is the essence of alignment. *Alignment is the arrangement of all ministries and staff around the same simple process.*

Builder Brooks

Herb Brooks built a great team. He did so by arranging all of the players not only around the same vision of winning a gold medal but also around the same approach to hockey.

You are a builder as well. It is not enough to unite the church around the same *what* (purpose), but they also must be aligned on the same *how* (process).

Imagine if you were building a house. If the team of contractors and builders agreed only on *what* was being built, you would have a problem. They would also need to be unified on the approach, on the plan. Otherwise the contractors and builders would be competing with one another for time, money, and scheduling preference.

The team must also rally around the *how*.

Without alignment, complexity is assured. Without alignment, you will not be simple. The church must be united around the same approach to ministry. The church must be aligned around the simple ministry process.

According to our research, there is a highly significant relationship between church vitality and alignment. In this chapter you will be given five essentials to alignment. All five flow from the research data.

If you want to maximize everyone's energy, you must recruit on the process, offer accountability, implement the same process everywhere, unite leaders around the process, and ensure that new ministries fit.

1: Recruit on the Process

Herb Brooks carefully selected players to be on the team. He looked for players who would be more committed to the name on the front of the jersey (USA) than the name on the back. After he chose his team, some insisted that the best players were missing. His response, as depicted in *Miracle*, is a classic line. He said, "I am not looking for the best players. I am looking for the right ones."

Brooks was looking for players who would align to the same approach to hockey. The right players are vital. Without the right leaders, the church will never be aligned. People follow leadership, and if leadership is not moving in the same direction, then people are scattered. Leaders are responsible to establish and reinforce the culture of the church. Consequently, if the leaders are not aligned, the church will not enjoy unity.

Sometimes the best players are not the right players.

Remember First Church. They hired "the best" for each role and found themselves with a divided staff. Theologically the team was aligned, but philosophically they were divided. Staff members used the same ministry jargon, but their approaches to ministry were often in conflict.

According to our research, it is vital that you recruit and hire people based in part to their commitment to your ministry process. It is critical that you hire and place leaders in key positions who are deeply committed to your simple ministry process. They must be committed not only to ministry but also to *how* your church does ministry.

We asked vibrant and comparison church leaders about the role their ministry process plays in recruiting leaders. We asked them to state their level of agreement with the following statement: "We recruit and hire leaders who are committed to our process."

The percentage of vibrant church leaders who recruit based on commitment to the ministry process was much greater than the percentage of comparison church leaders. Of the vibrant churches, 64 percent strongly agreed or agreed with the statement compared to 33 percent of the comparison churches.

Churches that bring people on the team who are committed to their simple process are enjoying the power of alignment. Everyone's energy is moving in the same direction.

A Funny/Sad Story

Eric and several of his friends (JR, Jorge, and Jeff) posted a fake advertisement on churchstaffing.com as a joke. Now churchstaffing.com is a serious site. In fact, it is the premiere site for churches seeking a staff member and leaders looking for a place of ministry. It is a great service; it is just that Eric and his buddies were bored one day. Actually, Eric is still trying to convince people it was "research."

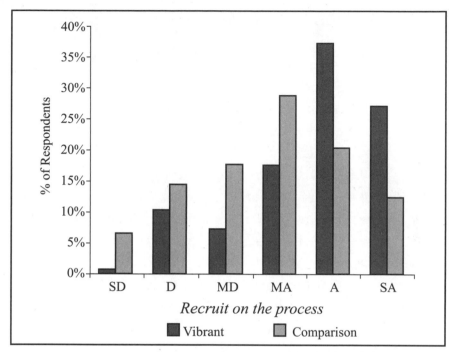

Figure 1. Respondents' level of agreement with recruiting on the process

Note: SD = Strongly disagree; D = Disagree; MD = Moderately disagree;
MA = Moderately agree; A = Agree; SA = Strongly agree

So they each pitched in forty bucks and pretended to be leaders from "Main Event Church." They were searching for a "Pastor of Extreme Worship Arts." Neither the church nor the position really existed, but they thought it would be fun to see if anyone responded. Here is how the ad read:

Main Event Church is seeking an exceptional leader to be our Pastor of Extreme Worship Arts. We believe the right person will be a unique fit for such a time as this. This person will serve under the Senior Pastor and will oversee all areas of worship. Candidates must embrace the Senior Pastor's vision of aligning all people of all denominations under the same vision. The person must also meet these requirements:

   –Ability to infuse the TULIP doctrine in all worship sets

   –Postmodern, Visionary, Missional leader capable of creating an ethos and apostolic movement in an Ancient-future church

   –Willing to find some songs written from a premillenial dispensationalist theological tradition

   –Desires to develop an emerging handbell choir

   –Some snake handling may be appropriate (for our believers service only)

   –Agree that the Lord is to be worshipped through magnificent attire and appropriate versions of the Bible

   –Demonstrate proof of a second blessing. Tongue speaking in various accents is a major plus as we are a multicultural church

   –Exegetically establish a movement of fluidity in the Extreme Worship Ministry

   We realize that many of these requirements are personal preferences and not biblical mandates. Therefore, each candidate must be aligned with roughly 3/4 of all our requirements.

   Please send a resume in Microsoft Word or Adobe Reader Format to James at maineventchurch@yahoo.com

The e-mail address was valid so that responses could be read. JR even built a temporary Web site for Main Event Church. The site said "Main Event Church: under construction." On the site was a picture of a young guy with long hair wearing a suit and holding a coat hanger. Attached to the coat hanger was a big random photograph of a snake. It could not have been more ridiculous.

The advertisement and Web site created quite a buzz. E-mails poured in from people applauding the humor of the ad. It was highlighted and discussed in numerous blogs (online journals). The link to the advertisement circulated throughout the country. We know this widespread circulation was real because it was forwarded to members of Eric's staff from people who did not know the origin of the ad.

That is the funny part of the story.

The sad part is that lots of people really applied. With real resumes and cover letters. Real people responded and asked for job descriptions. Some even sent in DVDs of themselves leading worship. We were shocked.

It is sad. Here is why. To apply for the position a person would have to: (1) have no basic theological belief system that guides his/her ministry or (2) be willing to compromise his/her beliefs in order to get a ministry job.

The person described in the advertisement does not exist. The theological tenets placed in the want ad oppose one another at the most basic level. We do not believe there is such a thing as a Calvinist (TULIP) who handles snakes. We do not believe there is such a thing as a leader who claims to be postmodern and traditional (magnificent attire and handbells). A premillenial dispensationalist who insists on a specific Bible translation would unlikely speak of creating an emerging ethos.

Eric and his buddies intentionally crafted the advertisement to contain opposing theological labels under the banner of Christianity. If a person claimed to ascribe to all of the thinking in the advertisement, he or she would be a schizophrenic believer. The person would lack a coherent belief system. Or worse, the person would be willing to subscribe to any belief system in order to land an interview.

Yet people applied. (By the way, Thom wanted to express his cowardice by disclaiming any involvement in this prank.)

This joke speaks to the seriousness of effectively recruiting and hiring people. It seems that some people are willing to believe anything to secure a job interview. If people are willing to subscribe to any belief system to be considered for a job, they will also be willing to subscribe to any ministry philosophy. If people are willing to compromise in the area of personal theology, they will also be willing to compromise in the area of ministry approach.

It is tragic. Churches need leaders who are deeply committed to a core belief system. Theological alignment among leaders in the same church is important. This alignment does not mean that the leadership team has all the answers or agrees on every passage or thought about God. However, they should be in sync on major theological doctrines.

While theological alignment is critical, so is philosophical alignment. Key leaders must be aligned to the same philosophy of ministry. If not, the church will move in a multiplicity of directions, driven by varying ministry philosophies.

Your simple ministry process is part of your ministry philosophy. It is *how* ministry is done at your church. Therefore, you should reference your simple ministry process as you hire and recruit. You should surface it early in the interviewing process. Use it to evaluate if potential leaders are a good fit with the direction of your ministry. You should recruit people who are not just accepting of your simple ministry process, but are deeply committed to it.

First, recruit on process. Second, offer accountability to leadership.

2: Offer Accountability

Once you have recruited staff or volunteers, you must lead them. One important aspect of leadership is accountability. It is especially critical to alignment. Without accountability, people naturally drift away from the declared ministry process.

Max Depree once stated, "Movements suffer when leaders are unwilling to hold the group accountable."[1] The church must be a movement, a movement that the gates of hell will not be able to stop (Matt. 16:18). The church must not just be a building, a creed, or an institution. The church is alive. The church is a movement of grace. And this movement suffers without accountability.

Church leaders must avoid the two extremes of micromanagement and neglect. Micromanagement stifles creativity and hampers shared leadership. Neglect fosters complacency and leads to a fragmented team.

The balance is good leadership. Leaders should outline the simple process but then allow ministry leaders to implement with freedom and creativity.

According to our research, offering accountability based on the simple process is important. We asked vibrant and comparison church leaders to evaluate the accountability they provide concerning the implementation of the process. We asked them to state their level of agreement with the following statement: "Our staff/leaders are held accountable for how the church process is implemented in their respective areas."

Of the vibrant church leaders, 55 percent strongly agreed or agreed with this statement compared to 31 percent of the comparison church leaders. In general, the vibrant church leaders are much more likely to hold people accountable to implement the simple ministry process.

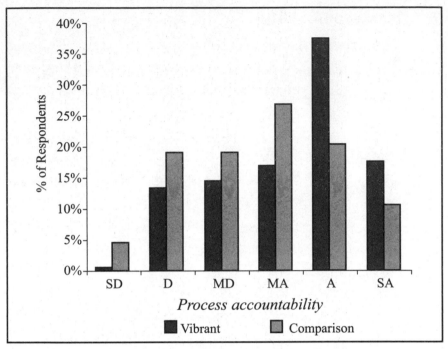

Figure 2. Respondents' level of agreement with process accountability
Note: SD = Strongly disagree; D = Disagree; MD = Moderately disagree;
MA = Moderately agree; A = Agree; SA = Strongly agree

While offering accountability is beneficial to the team and the entire church, it is intimidating for many church leaders. While people long for feedback and direction from their leaders, most church leaders are reluctant to offer it. Many church leaders admit it is an area in which they struggle.

Accountability does not need to be painful for either side of the equation. It can be liberating. It opens lines of communication for honest dialogue and produces some great conversations about ministry direction. As you consider offering accountability to those you lead (staff or volunteers), the following tool may prove helpful.

A Tool for Accountability

When Eric first became an executive pastor, he was blessed to have godly men in vibrant churches mentor him. These men had served in the same role as Eric for many years. A few of them are third cousins of Noah. Not really, but they are getting old. A few are waiting for the large-print edition of this book.

One of the concepts that Eric learned from these men was providing accountability to leadership.

Eric implemented Ministry Action Plans (MAPs) with the staff at Christ Fellowship. The impact of MAPs on the leadership culture has been phenomenal. Staff members have a clear direction each year, and each person's goals are tied to the simple ministry process. For those with a business background, MAPs are similar to the Management by Objectives system.

Peter Drucker developed the concept of Management by Objectives (MBO) in the 1950s. It is intended to be a tool that manages for results. Leaders and those they lead agree on measurable goals up front, and their agreement becomes the basis for evaluation. Each person sets his or her own goals based on the direction of the organization.[2]

At the beginning of each year, Eric sits down with each staff member to discuss his or her ministry action plan. The staff member comes to the meeting with a completed MAP. Each MAP includes how that specific ministry reflects the vision and process of the church, how the programs are designed to move people through the process, the organizational structure of the ministry, and a present evaluation of the ministry.

From these considerations each staff member sets five to seven measurable goals for the new ministry year. The staff member also outlines how these goals will be accomplished.

The MAPs force individual ministry goals to be related to the overall ministry process. Each person has a clear focus.

Throughout the year the status and progress of the goals are evaluated. They provided ongoing accountability that is not awkward. It is natural because things have already been written down. Staff members enjoy the feedback because they want to know where they stand.

The MAPs also align the entire team. Each staff member presents his goals to the entire staff. The staff gathers around the individual and prays for his or her ministry year. Each person knows what the others are doing. Everyone sees how the overall ministry process is being pursued in each ministry division. It creates energy. Each person sees that he or she is a part of the whole and that everyone is moving together in the same direction.

Recruit based on the simple process. Offer accountability for the implementation of the process. Implement the same process everywhere.

3: Implement the Same Process Everywhere

Where were you when it happened? Where were you when you realized that Gap is attempting to take over the world?

Surely, you have noticed.

There once was *the* Gap. One Gap. One store with men's and women's clothes. Great clothes at reasonable prices. Then the coup began to unfold . . . babyGap, GapKids, GapMaternity, and GapBody.

Gap is everywhere. Their stores are multiplying. Conspiracy theorists, be on guard.

Gap has chosen to appeal to different groups of people at various stages of life. However, they have done so under the same banner. Gap targets many different people under the same name and philosophy.

No matter which type of Gap store you walk into, you will see the same logo. You will see a similar store design and layout. You will be treated with the same type of customer care. And you can purchase items on your one Gap card. Therefore, no matter which type of store you choose to visit, you still know you are at the Gap.

Gap has expanded the number of people they influence while remaining simple. They have placed all services under the same identity. They have been able to grow while fighting for simplicity. They are still known and recognized simply as the Gap.

This is the power of alignment. That is the power of implementing the same process everywhere.

The church seeks to influence multiple groups of people at different stages of life. The church consists of children, teenagers, young adults, middle-aged adults, and seniors. What does alignment look like in a local church?

A church that is committed to alignment implements the same process everywhere. The simple ministry process guides each ministry department in the church. For example, the children's ministry, youth ministry, and young adult ministry have the same process as the entire church.

Each department, like the different versions of Gap, offers age-appropriate content and design. Each department implements a relevant version of the process for that particular age group. While the process is the same, each ministry area executes it with creativity and age-specific focus.

According to our research, integrating the same simple process into the entire culture of the church is wise. Integrating the same process in each ministry department makes a profound impact.

We asked the vibrant and comparison church leaders if they have the same ministry process in each ministry area. We asked them to state their level of agreement with the following statement: "While the styles and methods vary in different ministry departments (such as children and youth), the process is the same" (Figure 3).

Of the vibrant churches, 54 percent strongly agreed or agreed with the statement compared to 30 percent of the comparison churches. The percentage of vibrant churches that have the same process in all areas is significantly higher than the percentage of comparison churches that do.

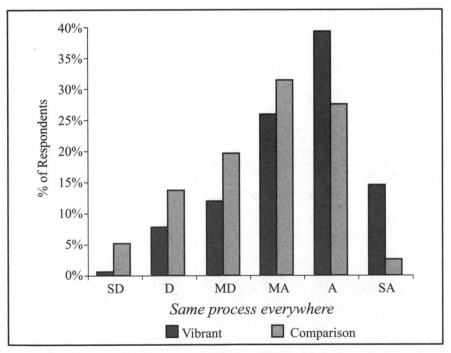

Figure 3. Respondents' level of agreement with same process everywhere
Note: SD = Strongly disagree; D = Disagree; MD = Moderately disagree;
MA = Moderately agree; A = Agree; SA = Strongly agree

The Benefits

Cross Church, from chapter 2, provides an excellent example. Cross Church's vision statement is, "Love God, love others, serve the world." To promote alignment, they have fully integrated the same process into every major department in the church.

The guiding direction of the children's ministry is to lead children to love God, love others, and serve the world. The guiding direction of the youth ministry is to lead students to love God, love others, and serve the world. The vision statement for the singles' ministry is to lead young adults to love God, love others, and serve the world.

There are at least three benefits of implementing the same process everywhere.

First, understanding is increased. An observer of Cross Church's ministry integrated process might say, "But that is the same thing for each area. It sounds so redundant."

Alignment is redundant in a good way.

Everyone at Cross Church understands the direction of each ministry department. It is simple. It is the same process everywhere. If you are an adult who understands the ministry process of the adult ministry, you also understand the ministry process of the children's ministry.

The alternative is complexity. Let's be honest: do you really think people know the ten to twelve different vision statements at complex churches? Our observation is that the leaders do not even know them. The people just ignore them. It is too complex.

Second, unity is promoted. Implementing the same process everywhere prevents the church from having multiple directions. A process that is fully implemented pulls each ministry department together. The alternative leads to a group of sub-churches that do not reflect the overall direction of the church.

Third, families experience the same process. Age-specific departments such as children, youth, and adults are responsible for the spiritual development of that particular age group. The leaders of those departments are responsible to design a process that brings those individuals to spiritual maturity. When each department implements the same process, families benefit.

Each family member experiences the same ministry process. Each member of a family is challenged to move through the same process. As people age and progress through the ministry departments, they are accustomed to the simple process. It creates synergy for the church and for the family.

At Cross Church each ministry department uses small groups to connect people relationally, to lead people to love others. Each member of a family is being challenged to grow in their love for others by joining a small group. When a father chooses to move to a small group, there will be one available for his son as well. When any member of a family moves to a small group, the rest of the family will be exposed to the next step in the process. Each ministry department is complementing the other ministry department.

That is the power of alignment.

Recruit and offer accountability based on your simple process. Implement in each ministry department. And unite people around the simple process.

4: Unite around the Process

One of the coolest toys for children is Mr. Potato Head. Mr. Potato Head has holes all over his body. The child gets to plug the body parts into the holes on Mr. Potato Head's body. The arms, feet, nose, eyes, ears, and lips are all placed in a specific spot on the body. When assembled the right way, Mr. Potato Head almost looks human. Almost.

Mr. Potato Head does not always look human though. Most children decide to place the body parts in different locations on his body. An arm will go where the nose is to be. The eyes will be placed where the feet belong. The nose will be attached to the side of poor Mr. Potato Head's face.

Sadly, most churches look like a discombobulated Mr. Potato Head. Everything is badly mixed up. The parts of the body are not aligned as they should be. Confusion abounds. While it is funny on the toy, it is not funny for churches.

Scripture refers to the church as Mr. Potato Head. Well not exactly, but close.

Scripture refers to the church as the body of Christ. When the body of Christ is working right, it is beautiful to behold. All of the parts are in the proper place. They are functioning in the right way. And they realize they are a part of the same one body (1 Cor. 12:12).

When the body is not united, it is not a pretty picture. Imagine when you tried to walk, if one leg went to the right and the other to the left. Imagine the confusion if your right eye looked up and your left eye looked down. Imagine the discomfort if your right arm refused to partner with your left arm. Imagine the perplexity if your feet decided not to operate with the rest of your body.

When a local body of Christ is not united in the same direction, the body is ineffective. When one part of the body refuses to function, there is disarray. When one part of the body wants to be a separate body, there is division. The world watches this and is confused.

The simple ministry process provides a framework for leaders in the church to rally around. The process can be used to unite the body. There is a clear direction, and each person has a place to plug into it.

According to our research, using your ministry process to bring focus to your leaders is beneficial. We asked vibrant and comparison church leaders if they use their ministry process to unite and focus their leaders. We asked them to state their level of agreement with the following statement: "Our process is the unifying factor that keeps all our leaders focused" (Figure 4).

Of the vibrant churches, 42 percent strongly agreed or agreed with this statement compared to 17 percent of the comparison churches. The vibrant church leaders are nearly three

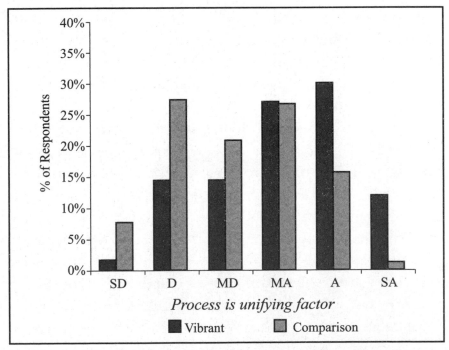

Figure 4. Respondents' level of agreement with process as unifying factor

Note: SD = Strongly disagree; D = Disagree; MD = Moderately disagree;
MA = Moderately agree; A = Agree; SA = Strongly agree

times as likely than the comparison church leaders to use the ministry process to bring focus to the leaders.

The Reality

Churches are filled with a variety of generations, nationalities, preferences, and backgrounds. Thankfully, most churches do not have uniformity. Uniformity is boring, and uniformity is different from unity. Athletic teams wear the same uniforms and may be divided.

Unity is much deeper than uniformity.

In fact, unity is best expressed in the midst of diversity. That is when it is clear that God is the one uniting people. Ultimately unity is found in Christ; however, the simple ministry process is a great tool to keep people on the same page.

In reality, Christ's followers have argued and disagreed for centuries. Differences in beliefs, both major and minor, have separated believers. However, more often in churches, the differences that lead to division are not theological or biblical. The differences that harm most churches are in the realm of ministry approach and philosophy.

People will often agree theologically but disagree about ministry philosophy. People will often nod their heads in agreement about a biblical issue but be diametrically opposed over a specific approach to ministry.

You have heard it, "Why are we doing it this way?" "Why are we not doing this anymore?" These are not theological issues; these are debates over preference, style, and approach.

Using your simple process as a unifying factor brings philosophical alignment. It helps leaders agree at the level where disagreement most often festers. It helps people be of the same mind in regards to ministry approach. In other words, leaders agree on *how* ministry is done at your church.

A simple church design is a philosophy of ministry. A simple church is *a congregation designed around a straightforward and strategic process that moves people through the stages of spiritual growth*. When people commit not only to the doctrinal beliefs of a church but also to the simple and strategic process, the energy of everyone is unleashed.

So while we embrace the reality that Christ is the giver of unity, we know that a simple ministry process may be used to unite people. The process of the church should become a point of agreement where people understand the overall picture and *how* ministry is accomplished. In order to keep leaders focused on the simple ministry process, you must remind them of the process and highlight their contributions to it.

Remind people of the process. The statement, "People need to be reminded more than instructed" is true. People tend to forget the direction of the church. Reminding people of the God-given process the church has embraced is necessary.

Remind people by tying ministry decisions or direction to the simple process. At General Electric, Jack Welch attempted to connect every decision to the direction of the company. By doing so, he reinforced the direction of the company.[3] At your church, all of the important details such as hiring, budgeting, facility changes, and building projects must be connected to the process God has given your church.

Highlight contributions to the process. Show leaders how they are contributing to the fulfillment of the ministry process. It takes the body operating properly for the simple ministry process to be realized. Show people how their seemingly small act of service is part of the big picture God is painting in your church.

Walk around. A lot. Management expert Edward Deming coined the phrase MBWA—Management by Walking Around. It is effective. Do ministry by walking around.

Walk around and remind people they are a part of the whole. The greeters fit into the process. Without the preschool workers, adults would not be able to move through the process of discipleship. The building and grounds teams prepare the facility so some aspect of your ministry process can happen. Tell them what it is, and thank them.

When people understand the vital part of the body they occupy, they will be more likely to unite to the whole. Without their commitment, the body of Christ would look like a three-year-old's version of Mr. Potato Head.

To maximize everyone's energy you must recruit according to the simple process, offer accountability for the implementation of the process, implement the same process in each ministry department, and unite people around the simple process. Finally, you must ensure that new ministries clearly fit into the overall design.

5: New Ministry Alignment

If you have ever designed a room or redecorated a house, you know that it is much easier to work with new furniture. You buy furniture with the room in mind. If it does not fit into the design of the room, you do not get it. The challenging part is figuring out where your existing furniture and pictures fit.

The same is true for alignment.

The most challenging aspect of alignment is pulling existing ministries and existing staff in the same direction, especially if they have been moving in opposite directions. It is much easier to align new people and new ministries to the overall direction.

If they do not fit, you simply do not allow them to begin.

According to our research, it is vital that you make sure new ministries fit into the simple process before they begin. Afterwards it is too late.

We asked vibrant and comparison church leaders to state their level of agreement with the following statement: "Before we begin a new ministry, we ensure that it fits within our process" (Figure 5).

Of the vibrant churches, 68 percent strongly agreed or agreed compared to 40 percent of the comparison churches. The vibrant church leaders tend to ensure new ministries understand their place in the process prior to their launch.

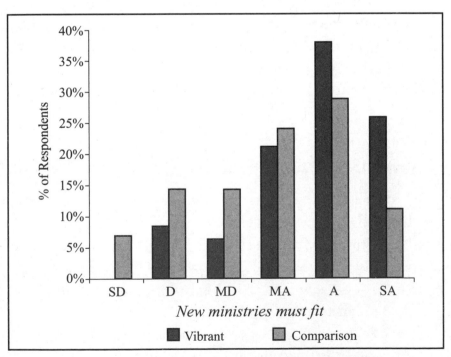

Figure 5. Respondents' level of agreement with new ministries fitting

Note: SD = Strongly disagree; D = Disagree; MD = Moderately disagree;
MA = Moderately agree; A = Agree; SA = Strongly agree

Checking the Fit

Before you purchase a new pair of shoes, you wear them in the store. You walk around in them. It would be unwise to buy them without knowing if they fit right. Shoes that do not fit are found at the bottom of your closet. They create more clutter. Checking the fit is essential.

Simple church leaders check the fit. Before a new ministry is launched, they ensure it is a viable part of the simple ministry process. They clarify specifically how the new ministry will move people through the process. And they ensure that the leaders of the new ministry understand how the ministry is part of the big picture.

We are drawing a distinction between a program and a ministry. In the next chapter you will be encouraged to be cautious about adding new programs to the ministry process. In fact, you will be challenged to eliminate some programs.

Ministries are different from programs. Ministries are either entire departments (see ministry expansions) or specific groups (see ministry additions) that help move people through one aspect of the process.

In a simple church new ministries can be divided into two broad categories: ministry expansions and ministry additions. Checking the fit prior to inception is critical for both.

Ministry expansions are new ministries that are geared toward a specific age group or life stage. The church ministry is expanding to focus intentionally on a specific group of people. The new ministry is going to be a new department within the church such as a new middle-school ministry department or young couples department. In both of these cases, these groups were formerly a part of a different ministry. Now they will have their own identity.

For ministry expansions, begin the new ministry with the same simple process. Be sure the programs within this ministry are placed to move people through the process. Ministry expansions are a great opportunity to highlight the simple process. You can begin them without the clutter. You can use these new ministries to show existing ministries the benefits of a streamlined approach.

Ministry additions are new ministries that fulfill a specific function within the simple process. These ministries must be set up to help move people through the process of transformation. For example, the baptism ministry team makes it easy for people to move to baptism. The guest reception ministry helps move guests into the life of the church. If it is unclear how a ministry addition will move people through the simple process, do not launch it.

A Lot Is at Stake

A lot was at stake for the *Miracle* hockey team. They were playing for a gold medal and the pride of a nation. Unity was essential. For them to reach their potential and realize their goal, alignment was not an option.

Alignment is essential for the church as well. And more is at stake.

There once was a group of people who were facing a stronger and bigger opponent than the Russian hockey team. The group of people was the Israelites, and the land of Canaan was at stake. Here is what happened.

The Israelites were the people God had chosen to love. They were slaves in Egypt for four hundred years. They dreamed about being released and being free. God raised up a leader named Moses to lead His people out of Egypt, out of bondage. God told Moses that He had set aside a special land for them called Canaan, which was to be theirs.

God's agenda was to get His people to Canaan, a land that He described as being full of milk and honey, an abundant land. This agenda was bigger than any game. It was their life and the lives of their families for generations to come.

God sent ten plagues to Egypt so that the Egyptian leader, the Pharaoh, finally told Moses to leave. But after letting them go, the Egyptians decided to chase after the Israelites. The Israelites came to the Red Sea and had nowhere to turn. God divided the Red Sea so that they could walk through the middle of it. They looked back to see it crashing on top of the Egyptians who were chasing them. They saw God rescue them.

God then led them on the way to Canaan. He went ahead of them protecting them each step. They saw His presence in a visible way with a cloud by day and a fire by night. They saw Moses come down from meeting with God with his face glowing. They were hungry, and God provided quail and manna. They had never seen, tasted, or heard of this manna before. But each day God catered a meal for them.

With all that God had done and was actively doing, you would think the people would unite on God's agenda. You would think these people would align to the plan God had given them.

Instead, they complained. They grumbled about every-thing. They muttered about Moses and his wife. They com-plained about the food they were eating. It was not a pretty sight. Dissension never is.

God would get furious with them, but each time Moses begged God to forgive the people. Moses was always asking God to put up with the people. God did things to get their attention, but they refused to unite around the calling God had for them.

Now in Numbers 13, they are near the land that God has promised them. It is like the night before the big game. They are about to enter Canaan. Moses chooses twelve people, one from each tribe of Israel, to go spy out this land of Canaan. It was the first committee recorded in Scripture, and the results were not good.

The mission was not to determine whether or not to go into the land. God had already told them that this was the land. The mission was simply to explore it. They spied on the land for forty days. Unfortunately, this forty-day campaign was a bust.

They came back to give the report on what they saw. They said, "The land is full of milk and honey, but." "But we also see the opponents, the other team. They are huge. We are like grasshoppers in their eyes."

Two of the spies, Joshua and Caleb, insist the land can be taken. "We can do it." But the other ten spread what the Bible calls an evil report. The report was not evil because it was false. It was not that they were spreading lies. The report was evil because of *how* they were spreading information. It was not what they were saying but *how* they were saying it.

The evil report spread among the entire camp like wildfire. That night, the people wanted to stone Moses and Aaron. They cried and said, "It would be better if we just died here in the desert than to go and die by the sword in the land of Canaan." That night was the defining moment for this fragmented team. Moses, again, begs God to forgive the people. Here is God's response:

The LORD responded, "I have pardoned them as you requested. Yet as surely as I live and as the whole earth is filled with the LORD's glory, none of the men who have seen My glory and the signs I performed in Egypt and in the wilderness, and have tested Me these 10 times and did not obey Me, will ever see the land I swore to give their fathers. None of those who have despised Me will see it. But since My servant Caleb has a different spirit and has followed Me completely, I will bring him into the land where he has gone, and his descendants will inherit it. Since the Amalekites and Canaanites are living in the lowlands, turn back tomorrow and head for the wilderness in the direction of the Red Sea."

Then the LORD spoke to Moses and Aaron: "How long must I endure this evil community that keeps complaining about Me? I have heard the Israelites' complaints that they make against Me. Tell them: As surely as I live, declares the LORD, I will do to you exactly as I heard you say. Your corpses will fall in this wilderness—all of you who were registered in the census, the entire number of you 20 years old or more—because you have complained about Me. I swear that none of you will enter the land I promised to settle you in, except Caleb son of Jephunneh and Joshua son of Nun. (Num. 14:20–30)

Wow! God says, "You want to die in the desert instead of going into the land of Canaan. Well, OK. Wish granted. Every one of you will die here in the desert."

What a tragic story. God had this phenomenal plan for His people. They were to enter into this special land. But they missed it. They missed God's best.

They refused to unite around the plan for their future that God had given them. They refused to trust and follow. Instead, they united around criticism, negativity, and dissension. And God took that very seriously.

He has always taken unity seriously. He still does.

God has a plan for the community of faith in which you are involved. A lot is at stake. Much more than a gold medal or an Olympic victory. Redemption. Eternity. Transformation. All of which are miracles.

Unity is essential.

The story is pretty gloomy, but it does have one bright spot—actually two. Caleb and Joshua. They had a different spirit, and they followed God wholeheartedly. They were willing to embrace God's agenda. They were willing to unite around God's plan. Therefore, God promised they would inherit the land of Canaan. And they did.

People must be challenged to be Calebs and Joshuas, to embrace wholeheartedly what God is doing in your church. People must be challenged to unite, to align to the simple process He has given your church.

A lot is at stake.

GROUP DISCUSSION QUESTIONS

1. Describe the best team experience you have ever had. What made it so special?
2. How have you seen disunity harm a church?
3. Why is unity around a ministry approach important?

4. On a scale of one to ten, how aligned is our leadership around our simple ministry process?
5. How comfortable are we with accountability?
6. What would "the same process everywhere" mean to our programming?

EIGHT

Focus: Saying No to Almost Everything

Art is a process of elimination. The sculptor produces the beautiful statue by chipping away such parts of the marble block as are not needed.

~ ELBERT HUBBARD

Clarity ➤➤ Movement ➤➤ Alignment ➤➤ Focus

As you can tell, both of us enjoy research. We love truth, and research seeks to discover truth. Research brings clarity to thinking and forces recommendations to be based on objective facts rather than causal observation or anecdotal wisdom.

One recent research project caught the attention of hundreds of thousands of Americans, the movie industry, and the fast-food restaurant industry. The recent research project was qualitative in nature and built upon an in-depth experimental research model. The documentary film chronicling the experiment is destined to be a cult classic.

We are talking about *Super-Size Me*.

Perhaps you were expecting something a bit more serious. You will not find *Super-Size Me* in the libraries of an academic institution or the annals of research journals. However, you can pick a copy up of this film at your local Blockbuster or order it through your Netflix account. While the film is a bit satirical, the results of the research are compelling, interesting, and appalling.

Super-Size Me is a low-budget independent documentary about the impacts of eating fast food consistently. Morgan Spurlock was the researcher and the producer of the film. He documented a monthlong experiment with McDonalds.

For an entire month all Spurlock ate was food from the golden arches. The film takes you, the viewer, on the monthlong eating adventure.

You observe the results unfolding as you watch the movie. You are on the journey with the McDonalds-driven life. Thirty days of processed food. Devotionals not included.

Spurlock had three rules in his experiment. First, he had to accept supersize portions if they were offered. They often were, and for only forty cents who can blame his indulgence? Second, he could only eat what is available on the McDonalds menu. Nothing else could enter his body, not even a Tic Tac. Third, he had to eat every item on the menu at least once.

This would be a dream month for most kids. So what were the results?

Spurlock began the study weighing 185 pounds, athletic, and healthy. He did not remain so. He gained twenty-five pounds in one month. He began to suffer from fatigue, headaches, and indigestion. His body basically fell apart over the course of the McDiet. His blood sugar skyrocketed. His liver filled with fat. His cholesterol went off the charts, and his blood pressure was unmanageable.

Since viewing the movie, Eric has not eaten fast food. (*Thom's note*: He insists pizza is not fast food.) The results of Spurlock's experiment are clear. They confirm what we already knew, but seeing the extreme results is alarming.

The conclusion: Fast food is not healthy.

In fact, many doctors believe it is killing Americans. The appropriate response: Say no to fast food.

The menu at fast-food restaurants has continually expanded. More and more types of food are offered. The sizes have also increased. What was once a regular order of fries is now a child-size order in many establishments.

We, the consumers, are to blame. We like food, and we like it fast. We have developed taste buds for fries dipped in grease and burgers cooked in masses. Fast-food establishments are simply capitalizing on our poor choices. Our tastes and our busy lives have expanded the menus . . . and our waistlines.

And we keep getting more and more unhealthy.

Spiritual Super-Size Me

There is an epidemic of fast-food spirituality among believers today. We like big spiritual menus with lots of options. And we want those options served to us fast.

Many churches have become like fast-food establishments. A new idea emerges, and the menu is expanded. Someone wants a special event served a particular way, and the menu is expanded. People assume the more that can be squeezed into the menu, the better. So the brochure, the week, the calendar, the schedule, and the process get expanded. Cluttered.

And we keep getting more and more unhealthy.

One would think that the more programs and the more special events that are offered, the greater the impact. Our research has confirmed that the opposite is true. Unfortunately, the big and expanding menus are not producing vibrant churches.

The conclusion: fast-food spirituality is not healthy. In fact, the large and fast menu approach to ministry is killing our churches.

The appropriate response: Stay focused on your simple process. Say no to everything else.

If you follow the input given in this book, you will begin designing a simple process for ministry. It will be clear, and it will move people toward spiritual maturity. You will also align all of your people and your ministries around this process.

Then the hard part will begin, and it will never end. It will be ongoing for the rest of your ministry life.

Focus.

As we have said from the beginning, this factor is the most difficult simple church element to implement and practice. It means saying no a lot.

Saying no is difficult. No church leader wants to be perceived as David Spade on the Capital One commercials. You have seen those commercials, the ones where Spade says no to every question, to every call. Church leaders do not want to be that guy.

Church leaders have feelings. Well, most of them do. Seriously, most have the heart of a pastor who cares deeply for the people they serve. Saying no is difficult because it tends to bother the person who hears it. While it may be difficult, our research indicates that it is necessary.

Saying no must be done with God's wisdom and timing. You must remember that you are dealing with people who have feelings.

Staying focused is essential to being simple, and a church cannot stay focused without saying no. While it is not easy, the health of the church is at stake. We must boycott fast-food spirituality. We must focus.

One Thing

Focus is a truth taught and affirmed throughout Scripture. The focus of individuals in the Bible is humbling, and the principle of *one thing* emerges.

David prayed in Psalm 27:4, "I have asked one thing from the LORD; it is what I desire: to dwell in the house of the LORD all the days of my life." One thing was his focus. An intimate and passionate relationship with God consumed him.

Paul said in Philippians 3:13–14, "But one thing I do: forgetting what is behind and reaching forward to what is ahead, I pursue as my goal the prize promised by God's heavenly call in Christ Jesus." One thing was his focus. The goal of Christlikeness compelled him to move forward in his spiritual journey. In fact, for Paul, everything else was filth compared to this one thing (Phil. 3:8).

Paul instructed Timothy to train himself to be godly. To do so, Timothy would have to avoid all the godless chatter and legalistic principles surrounding him. He had to focus on the one thing of being transformed by God (1 Tim. 4:7–8).

The writer of Hebrews instructs us to throw off sin and everything else that hinders us from running the race that Christ has marked out for us (Heb. 12:1). Runners would not run a race wearing a fur coat or ankle weights. Runners do run a race with streamlined and simple clothing. Everything else is tossed.

The writer of Hebrews issues a call to focus, to fix our eyes only on Christ (Heb. 12:2). One thing. The challenge is to get rid of anything that gets in the way of spiritual transformation.

As a church leader, you partner with God to build the lives of people. If God has given you a clear process for making and maturing disciples, you must focus on this one thing in your church. Then people may run the race without ankle weights.

The Focus of a Builder

Remember, you are a builder.

Imagine sitting down with your family to design a house. You invest months in the designing process. There are so many decisions, so much to think about. You work hard to accommodate the wishes of everyone in the family.

The kids want their rooms a certain way and as far away from each other as possible. The sizes of the rooms are considered, the traffic flow throughout the house, where and how guests will be entertained, the back porch, the bathtub, the placement of the island in the kitchen, whether to have an island in the kitchen or not, and so on. After months of wrestling with the blueprints, you finally have a clear design.

Then you plan how the project will move, how it will progress. You work with a general contractor to set up the schedule of subcontractors who will come to work. They are placed strategically and in order. The project begins with people who will excavate the property and pour the foundation. The project ends with painters and installers. A lot happens in the middle. It is not an easy task.

Next you align all the resources and people to the plan. You ensure everyone knows the process and where he or she fits. You discipline yourself to work only with subcontractors who understand and are committed to the blueprints.

The project begins.

A few weeks into it, your daughter decides she does not like the location of her room. It is too close to the garage, and the garage door opening will wake her in the morning when you leave for work. She wants her room to be on the back of the house.

Your son is thinking of playing the drums. He was not into drums before the plans emerged, but he is now. At least he thinks he is. His room is far too small for a drum set, and your spouse informs you that there is no way the drums are going in the living room.

The project is in jeopardy. Everyone at one time signed off on it, but now other things are stealing focus. Drums, garage doors, life. It all happens.

You had a clear design, a project built to move, and everyone was aligned. Now it could all be lost. The clarity, movement, and alignment will mean nothing if you lose focus.

What do you do?

You will face the same dilemma as a builder of lives and a builder of the kingdom. After you have designed a simple church process with clarity, movement, and alignment, you are not done. There will be a constant temptation to abandon simplicity, to lose focus, to become cluttered.

What will you do?

According to our research, there is a highly significant relationship between church vitality and the church's focus on the process. In our study, churches that are single-minded when it comes to their ministry process were far more likely to be a vibrant and growing church.

You are a builder, and focus is mandatory. While clarity, movement, and alignment are essential, they are meaningless without focus. *Focus is the commitment to abandon everything that falls outside of the simple ministry process.* In this chapter you will be given five essentials to focus. All five are important and emerge from our research findings.

You must eliminate nonessential programs, limit adding more programs, reduce special events, and ensure the process is easy to communicate and simple to understand.

1: Eliminate

Elimination. It is necessary, and it is also difficult.

It is especially difficult for pack rats. Pack rats are a type of rat that continually collects and transports junk. People who collect and hoard meaningless or worthless items are also referred to as pack rats.

If you have ever been in a pack rat's home, you have been shocked at the piles of magazines, newspapers, dishes, and random items. You found it difficult to make your way through the home. You have volunteered to help clean up, but the person insists that all the stuff is needed.

According to research, pack rats most likely suffered a brain lesion that damaged the part of the brain that keeps pack-ratting behavior in check. A study done at the University of Iowa on eighty-six pack rats discovered that each person had suffered some type of brain injury.[1] In other words, elimination is neurologically challenging for a pack rat.

Many churches are pack rats.

Many churches are littered with clutter. Floundering programs and ministries are stored and piled on top of one another. It is hard for people to make their way through the process of spiritual transformation because of the distracting clutter.

While elimination is not neurologically challenging for churches, it is interpersonally and historically challenging. People and history are involved. People lead these programs, and these programs have a history. Church leaders who desire to eliminate programs will inevitably offend the past or some individual.

While eliminating programs is difficult, the data indicates that vibrant church leaders have the discipline to do so. In other words, they are willing to clean out the clutter. Churches that eliminated programs were far more likely to excel in the focus element and be among the vibrant church groups.

We asked vibrant church leaders and comparison church leaders about their commitment to eliminate. We asked them to state their level of agreement with the following statement: "We seek to eliminate programs that do not fit in our process, even if they are good."

Of the vibrant churches, 46 percent strongly agreed or agreed with the statement compared to 22 percent of the comparison churches. Vibrant church leaders agreed or strongly agreed more than twice as much as the comparison leaders that they seek to eliminate programs that are not in the process (Figure 1).

Going Google

In chapter 1, you learned that Google's simplicity is dominating the market. People are attracted to their clutter-free search page. While YAHOO! and MSN have a huge cyberspace menu of options, Google has remained simple, and it is working.

As you read that, you may wonder why other search engine companies do not follow suit. Why are they not learning from Google's success and choosing to streamline their search engine Web pages? Why don't they just eliminate?

They can't. They can't stop being pack rats.

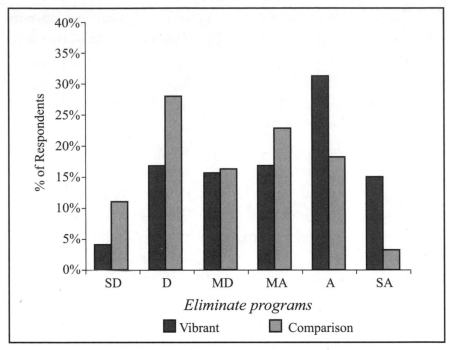

Figure 1. Respondents' level of agreement with eliminating programs

Note: SD = Strongly disagree; D = Disagree; MD = Moderately disagree;
MA = Moderately agree; A = Agree; SA = Strongly agree

At least that is what Google says. Marissa Mayer oversees the Google home page. She is responsible to keep it simple. She says that "once you have a home page like our competitors, paring it back like Google's is impossible. You have too many stakeholders who feel they should be promoted on the home page."[2]

So according to Mayer, it would be too painful to get simple. People who have paid money for their services to be on the home page would be upset. Going Google would be interpersonally and historically challenging. Going Google would cause a revolt, a mutiny.

Ouch.

Because of our belief in God's total provision, we do not believe it is impossible for a church to become simple. But it is difficult. It requires an absolute focus on the ministry process. This focus translates into forsaking programs that are outside of the ministry process.

It is not impossible because church leaders are called by God to be good stewards, and God makes the impossible possible. The bottom line is that elimination is a matter of being a faithful steward.

Stewardship

Since elimination is a matter of stewardship, it is a spiritual issue. Eliminating programs that are not in the simple ministry process is choosing to be wise with the time and resources God has given. It matters to God. And it should matter to us.

Ephesians 5:15–16 says, "Pay careful attention, then, to how you walk—not as unwise people but as wise—making the most of the time because the days are evil."

Paul had two words he could have used for "time" in this verse: *chronos* and *kairos*. *Chronos* refers to time in general. It is clock time and the root word for chronological. *Kairos* refers to a predetermined, specific amount of time. It is measured, allocated, and fixed.

Paul used *kairos*.

His word choice is huge. He was saying in essence, you have a specific amount of time here in this world. That is it. It is already set. It is fixed. The clock is ticking. Your time is running out. Even now.

So make the most of it. Don't just spend it. Invest it. Be wise. Be wise with the time God has given you. Eliminating programs, as God leads, is choosing to be wise stewards of the time and resources He has given.

Be a wise steward of time. Keeping programs that are not within the process is bad stewardship of your people's time. Their time is spent attending programs you have identified as being outside your ministry process. If elimination does not occur, people spend hours of time attending programs that are nonessential to your church's ministry process.

If these nonessential programs remain, your ministry process is diluted. It loses its power. Instead of promoting and discussing only the essential programs in your process, you find yourself promoting everything. The result is that people are scattered among a myriad of programs instead of committed to a focused few.

What is worse, people lose the impact of the essential programs to attend the nonessential ones. People in your church only have a certain amount of discretionary time, and they cannot afford to attend an abundance of weekly programs. If they are constantly invited and challenged to attend these nonessential programs, they miss the essential ones that are designed specifically to move them along the process of transformation.

Refusing to eliminate is also bad stewardship of your leaders' time. Instead of being able to focus on doing a few things with excellence, they lead a lot of programs with mediocrity.

Our observation is that simple churches exhibit excellence to a greater degree than complex churches. In most cases it is not that the leaders of complex churches lack a commitment to excellence. They simply cannot provide it with the number of programs they oversee. Their focus and attention is spread too thin. It is divided too much.

Be a wise steward of money. Keeping programs that are not within the process is also bad stewardship of resources. Money is spent funding programs that do not enhance the process. Most people do not see all the costs. Costs for staffing and pure ministry are obvious, but hidden costs such as printing and utilities exist as well.

And this money is important. Do not forget: the money is the tithes and offerings of the people. Instead of spending it on programs outside the process, invest it on programs within your ministry process. Those programs could be done with more excellence, if you gave them the money from the non-essential programs. As programs are eliminated, so are line items in your budget. And this elimination means more resources for your essential programs.

A Case Study from Eric's Church

The early childhood ministry at Christ Fellowship plays a huge role in the weekend services. Preschoolers are taught and parents are freed up to attend the services without distraction. To execute the weekends with excellence, the early childhood ministry had to narrow its focus. Elimination was necessary.

The early childhood ministry had formerly offered a Mothers Morning Out program twice a week. While this program was highly appreciated by mothers in the church, it was not an essential program in the ministry process. It took a tremendous amount of time for the early childhood staff to run the program. Instead of overseeing and recruiting volunteers for only the weekends and midweek program, staff also had to oversee this additional program.

Energy was divided, and the essential programs in the process were suffering. Several times families were turned away during the weekend services because there were not enough volunteers. Unintentionally, Mothers Morning Out competed with the weekend and midweek programs.

It had to be eliminated. This decision was both historically and interpersonally challenging.

Paid child-care workers who made additional income from Mothers Morning Out were frustrated with the decision, as were parents who loved the service. It was not easy. Some people still don't like Eric. Who can blame them?

However, the decision has made the early childhood ministry more effective. They are equipped to handle more kids on the weekend because their attention is less divided. The staff's time is more focused; therefore, the excellence factor is higher. Ultimately, parents appreciate the increased quality of the weekend early childhood ministry.

It may be time to say no to some of your nonessential programs.

Eliminate nonessential programs and then limit adding new ones.

2: Limit Adding

Our research indicates that in order to be focused, you must be careful not to add programs to the ministry process. Doing so would lengthen it; and the longer it is, the fewer people will be able to move through it. It will be an ongoing battle.

It is at Google.

Many people want to add links to their simple home page. As developers produce new services for Google such as maps, alerts, and scholarly papers, there is tremendous pressure to add links for these services to the home page. Marissa Mayer, known as the high priestess of simplicity, says, "I have to say no to a lot of people." Google's research tells them that people only remember seven to ten services on rival sites, so they offer six services on their home page.[3]

We asked vibrant and comparison church leaders about their reluctance to add programs to their ministry process.

We asked them to state their level of agreement with the following statement: "We use our existing weekly programs for special emphases/initiatives instead of adding new programs" (Figure 2).

The percentage of vibrant church leaders (58 percent) who agreed or strongly agreed that their church uses existing programs for special emphases instead of adding new programs was much greater than that of the comparison church leaders (39 percent). In general, vibrant churches are hesitant to add programs. Instead, they funnel needs and emphases through their existing programs. They do so because they view everything through their ministry process, and they do not want to alter it.

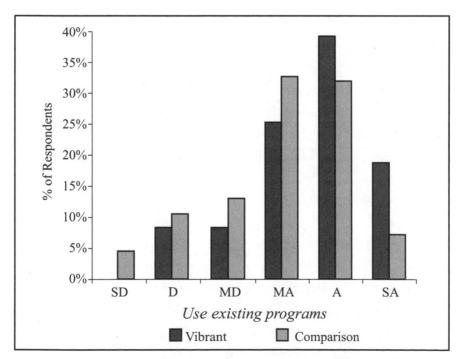

Figure 2. Respondents' level of agreement with using existing programs

Note: SD = Strongly disagree; D = Disagree; MD = Moderately disagree;
MA = Moderately agree; A = Agree; SA = Strongly agree

While the comparison churches are program-centered, the vibrant churches are process-centered. The comparison churches think about programs, so adding a new one is second nature. The vibrant churches think about the process, so being skeptical of an additional program is second nature. Adding a program would jeopardize their ministry design.

The Solution

So what do church leaders do when God burdens them with a specific need that must be addressed? What do church leaders do when God leads them to emphasize something to the entire church? Simple church leaders seek to meet the need through an existing program while complex church leaders add another program. Simple church leaders funnel special emphases through the existing programs in the process.

For example, if a church decides to emphasize stewardship, they are confronted with the dilemma of when to offer stewardship classes. The complex church leaders tend to add new classes to the church calendar. The entire church would be challenged to come to these classes. Many of these people are already involved in a group or class. Are they expected to come another night of the week or to drop out of their existing group? While the emphasis began with pure motives, it results in confused and overwhelmed church members.

Simple church leaders approach the stewardship emphases differently. Instead of starting a separate program, they offer the classes through their small group structures. People are given the opportunity to experience the stewardship emphasis in their existing groups, and people who are not yet in a group are challenged to join one. There is no new program, just a new focus.

By funneling the stewardship groups through the existing small-group structure, not only are people being exposed to the stewardship teaching, but they are also progressing through the simple ministry process. People who are not yet plugged into a group are challenged to join one of the new stewardship groups. Since the new groups are a part of one of the essential programs in the process, this simultaneously moves people along in the process.

The discipline to use existing programs allows leaders to provide constant promotion of the process and the programs within it. No time is wasted pushing programs that are outside the simple ministry process. Using existing programs protects the process from becoming too complicated. As the length and complication of the process increases, the number of people who are able to progress through the process decreases.

Simple church leaders have come to realize that less is more.

Less Is More

It is a counterintuitive statement and concept. Think about it. How is less ever really more? More should be more because *more* means "more." Most church leaders operate under the assumption that more is more. It seems logical to assume that more programs equal more impact. One would reason that churches that offer the most programming would be the most effective.

Travis Bradshaw from the University of Florida thought so. He thought more would be more. Then he conducted a research project on church growth. He originally hypothesized that churches that offered more programs would grow more than churches that offered fewer programs. His research proved the opposite.

The more programming the churches in Bradshaw's study offered, the less they grew. He placed churches in categories based on the number of programs they offered, and the churches that experienced the highest percentages of growth were the churches that offered fewer programs.[4]

Less really is more.

Less programs mean more focus on the programs offered. Less programs means more excellence. Less programs mean more energy for each program. Less programs mean more money allocated to each program. Less programs mean more people coming to the ones that are offered. Less programs mean more attention from the people in your church.

Less programs means more impact.

While we are advocating that you use existing programs, we are not suggesting that you never begin something new. New is great. New creates energy. New grabs attention. New produces growth. But new does not have to be more. New can be a part of less. There is a key distinction between a new program and a new option.

Options, Not Programs

When we say to limit adding, we are referring to programs. New options are necessary, and new options are not new programs. Add more options, not more programs. A new option is just an expansion of your present programming, and this is a big difference.

You must not miss this important distinction.

Adding new worship services or worship venues is not adding an additional program to your process. It is an expansion of your present programming. It is providing another option for your people. Adding new small groups is not an additional program; it is providing another opportunity for someone to engage in a small group. New small groups or Sunday school classes under the banner of your existing small groups or Sunday school structure is not another program. It is another option.

Are you asking people to come to more programs, or are you giving new options? Giving new options helps engage people who are not involved. It also frees up space, multiplies ministry, and provides energy. New tends to do that.

Think about this from the perspective of people in your church.

If you provide another worship service, would you expect people who are already plugged into a worship service to come to another service? If so, it is another program. If not, it is another option. If you provide small groups on another night, would you expect people already plugged into a group to come to another group? If so, it is another program. If not, then it is another option.

You should be prepared to say no to adding new programs to your process because your focus would be divided. However, you should be eager to add new options because new options help move more people through your simple ministry process.

Eliminate, limit adding programs, and reduce special events.

3: Reduce Special Events

If any athlete is known for focus, it is Michael Jordan.

In Jordan's latest book, *Driven from Within*, Fred Whitfield tells a fascinating story about Jordan's focus. Fred is a friend of Jordan, and one night Jordan and Fred were going out for the evening. Michael asked Fred if he could borrow a jacket.

In Fred's closet he had two main types of clothes: Nike and Puma. The Nike outfits came from his relationship with Jordan, and the Puma outfits came from his relationship with Ralph Sampson. Both athletes had lucrative endorsement deals with those respective companies: Jordan with Nike and Sampson with Puma.

Fred recalls that Jordan walked into the living room and laid all of the Puma gear on the floor. Jordan then went to the kitchen, grabbed a butcher knife, and returned to the living room. He proceeded to destroy all of the Puma clothes with the knife. He literally cut them to shreds, picked up the scraps, and carried everything to the dumpster.

Jordan came back inside and told Fred, "Don't ever let me see you in anything other than Nike. You can't ride the fence."[5]

That is good advice.

You cannot ride the fence. You must be focused. After you have designed your simple ministry process, all of your programming focus should go to executing the process. Our research indicates you should reduce the number of special events you produce and promote as a church.

Perhaps it is time to pull out the knife—figuratively speaking, of course.

We asked vibrant and comparison church leaders about their use of special events and conferences. We asked them to state their level of agreement with the following statement: "We limit the number of conferences and special events that we do as a church" (Figure 3).

Of the vibrant churches, 25 percent strongly agreed with this statement, while 6.0 percent of the comparison churches strongly agreed with this statement. The percentage of vibrant church leaders (57 percent) who agreed or strongly agreed that their church limits the number of conferences and special events they do as a church was much greater than that of the comparison church leaders (38 percent).

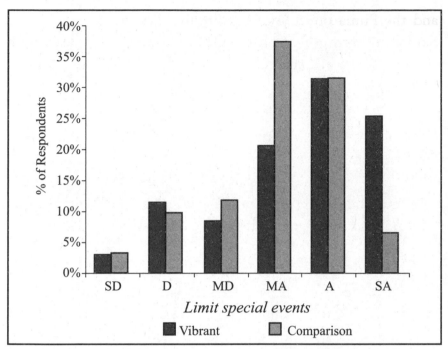

Figure 3. Respondents' level of agreement with limiting special events
Note: SD = Strongly disagree; D = Disagree; MD = Moderately disagree;
MA = Moderately agree; A = Agree; SA = Strongly agree

In general, simple churches are so focused on their ministry process that there is little time for extra events. Special events would get in the way. They would distract.

If special events are always publicized in a church, the essential programs that move people through the process are not properly emphasized. Moreover, the events compete with the essential programs for the time of the people.

Reducing special events is a challenge. Some special events can be beneficial to the church if they are used strategically. Following are three suggestions in regard to special events based on our observations of simple churches.

Funnel the Event into an Existing Program

Often a special event is planned to address a spiritual need in people's lives. And the solution offered for the need is an event. You have seen that happen. Events have become a way for leaders to address an issue quickly, and with little commitment. Providing an event is easier than walking with people through a situation.

In most cases the need can be better met through existing programming instead of a special event. And the ministry continues. It is more ongoing. Events are finished after the building is locked.

Think about your consultation with First Church and Cross Church (chapter 2). Both churches were burdened for marriages in their church, and rightly so. Both churches discovered curriculum they felt would impact families. It was the same curriculum.

First Church offered a two-day marriage seminar at their church. They promoted it heavily and had a low number of attendees. At the same time, their weekly programs were not a priority. Everything was about the seminar.

Cross Church acted differently. They offered numerous short-term small groups under the banner of their existing small-groups ministry. The same content was offered in conjunction with their simple ministry process. People received the teaching and at the same time were plugged into an essential program within the process.

At First Church, the seminar came and went. At Cross Church, the small groups have the option to continue. Relationships are still developing.

Same burden. Same content. Different approach. Different result.

Combine the Event with an Existing Program

In some situations, combining the special event with an existing program is more effective. Stacking a special event on top of an existing program gives new energy to the program. Instead of promoting and planning a special event and the existing program separately, the two complement each other. They are planned and promoted together.

Combining the event with an existing program also brings attention to the essential program. More people are invited and exposed to the essential program. This increases the likelihood that they will return. Following are some examples of combinations we have observed:

The traditional "dinner on the grounds" is a prime example of stacking a special event on top of an essential program. Instead of having a dinner for the entire church on a separate occasion as a stand-alone event, the dinner on the grounds is combined with the worship service. Traditionally, it is a big day. People are invited to stay after church for dinner, and during this time relationships are developed.

Christmas services are being combined with weekend worship services to maximize the potential of the holiday season. Instead of having a separate Christmas Eve or Christmas Day service in addition to a regular weekend service, churches have offered one special Christmas service multiple times over several days. By doing so, more people are exposed to a typical weekend service. In addition, all energy and publicity are focused on the one service that is offered multiple times.

Youth events are being combined with the entry-level program in youth ministry. Instead of having a fun event on a different night, youth ministries have combined the event with their regular entry-level program. Attention and work are focused on the same event/program, and new students are more likely to return because they have been exposed to the weekly program.

Children's harvest parties are being combined with the Saturday night worship service at several churches. Families are invited to stay for the Saturday evening service at the conclusion of the harvest party. The harvest party becomes a clear bridge to the worship service instead of just an event at a different time.

Use the Special Event Strategically

If the event cannot be funneled into or combined with an existing program, then it must be placed strategically along the simple process. There must be a "now what?" at the end of each event. A "now what?" means people are able to plug into an essential program at the conclusion of the event. The event should be used to move people to an essential program in the process.

For example, imagine that a church provides a parenting seminar. They decide to have a clear "now what?" at the conclusion of the seminar. They are prepared to offer new parenting groups to participants. Before people leave the event, they are encouraged to sign up for a group.

As you are eliminating, reducing, and limiting additional programs, you must continually bring attention to the simple ministry process. Therefore, you must be sure your process is easily communicated and understood.

4: Easily Communicated

Bringing focus to a church is not easy. A tension exists, a tension that must be held in balance.

On the one hand, the simple process will be understood more as you eliminate, use existing programs, and reduce special events. As you do these things, people will know you are serious. For some people the process will not be grasped until these bold moves are made. These bold moves will get attention, force discussion, and lead to understanding.

On the other hand, the process must be understood as these changes are made. If key leaders do not grasp the process in the midst of change, division is certain. As programs are eliminated and special events reduced, you must point people to the simple process. You must communicate.

In one sense the process will be understood more as these moves are made. In another sense the process must be understood before these moves are made. As a church leader, you must wrestle with this tension.

Since understanding is so critical, you must be comfortable articulating your process. As you eliminate and reduce special events, you will need to be constantly communicating the simple ministry process. To keep the church focused, you must regularly remind people.

According to our research, it is vital that your process be easy to communicate.

You must feel right as you say it. You must be able to preach it with conviction. The process must be part of who you are. If the ministry process is not easy to communicate, it will not be understood.

We asked vibrant and comparison church leaders to evaluate how easily they explain their ministry process. We asked them to state their level of agreement with the following statement: "Our process is easy to communicate" (Figure 4).

Of the vibrant churches, 56 percent strongly agreed or agreed with the statement compared to 24 percent of the comparison churches. Vibrant church leaders agreed or strongly agreed more than twice as much as the comparison leaders that their process is easy to communicate.

Simple church leaders are able to articulate their process, while complex churches struggle to do so. If you want people to understand why you are so passionate about your ministry process, you must be able to communicate it with ease. If you desire for people to agree with the single-minded focus of your church, your process must be easily articulated.

Key 5: Simple to Understand

According to our data, your process must be simple to understand. Your process must not only be simple on your side

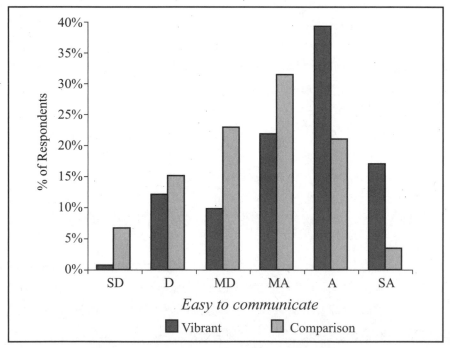

Figure 4. Respondents' level of agreement with the
process being easy to communicate

Note: SD = Strongly disagree; D = Disagree; MD = Moderately disagree;
MA = Moderately agree; A = Agree; SA = Strongly agree

of the communication equation, but it also must be simple for the hearer to grasp. People are incapable of focusing on something they do not understand. Understanding leads to focus and commitment.

People within a church are able to move through the process of spiritual transformation when they truly get it. So as a church leader, you must make sure your process can stick in the minds of your people. People should be able to nod their heads when they hear it.

It is vital that your process be understood because you will be saying no to everything else. No is easier to accept when the reasoning is clear. If people understand the commitment to the simple process, they will be more likely to embrace the decisions that accompany such focus.

We asked vibrant and comparison church leaders to evaluate how simple it is for people to understand their ministry process. We asked them to state their level of agreement with the following statement: "We have made our process simple for people to understand."

Of the vibrant churches, 50 percent strongly agreed or agreed compared to 24 percent of the comparison churches. Vibrant church leaders agreed or strongly agreed more than twice as much as the comparison leaders that they have made their process simple to understand (Figure 5).

Simple church leaders ensure the people in the church can understand their process. Making your process understandable requires simple language and brevity.

Choose simple language. Any word that has to be parsed or explained should not be used to describe your process. The description of your ministry process must be easy to understand. Carefully select the words and phrases.

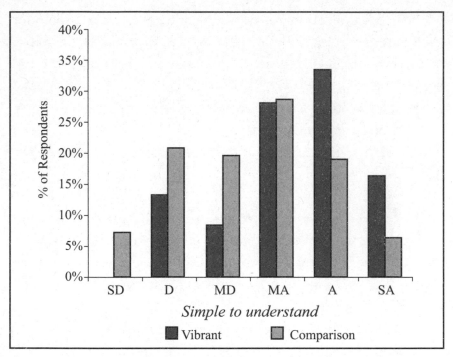

Figure 5. Respondents' level of agreement with process being understandable
Note: SD = Strongly disagree; D = Disagree; MD = Moderately disagree;
MA = Moderately agree; A = Agree; SA = Strongly agree

Be brief. The amount of information people are confronted with today is overwhelming. And it is increasing. It has been estimated that the world produced five exabytes of information in 2002. That is the same amount of information produced from the beginning of time through the year 2000.[6]

Obviously most of the information presented to people does not stick. We are on information overload. So be sure the description of your ministry process is brief. Brochures and written documentation about your process must be short, assuming you want people to read it. If multiple pages are needed to explain your process, go back to the drawing board.

Eliminate. Reduce. Limit additions. All will lead to greater focus. In the midst of the refocusing, your process must be communicated and understood.

Simple churches are focused. They say no to almost everything.

Just like great organizations.

Focus and Greatness

Great organizations are focused. They are good at saying no.

Apple, the designers and producers of the iPod and iMac, excel in simplicity because they are so focused. Steve Jobs, the leader of the organization, said he is "as proud of the things they have not done as he is of the things they have done."[7]

Did you catch that?

He is excited that Apple has said no. It has reaped great benefits.

Procter & Gamble is the largest manufacturer of household products in the United States. In the late 1990s P&G committed to simplicity. They felt they had become too complex. They decided to eliminate, to streamline. From 1996 to 1998 alone, they reduced the number of products by 20 percent. They sold some product lines to other companies and completely buried others.[8]

They began to say no a lot. And they accomplished more with less. Everyone knew that eliminating products would reduce costs, but it also bolstered sales. Market share increased by five points. Reducing clutter produced big results.[9]

When Jack Welch became the CEO of General Electric, he made a bold statement. GE would be number one or number two in every market, or they would eliminate that part of the business. They would focus only where they could be the best. They would say no to everything else.[10]

Just like great organizations, simple churches are focused. They say no.

Are you ready to say no?

Are you committed to staying focused on the simple ministry process?

GROUP DISCUSSION QUESTIONS

1. What programs are nonessential in our ministry process?
2. What prevents us from eliminating?
3. How could our approach to special events be altered?
4. Why is saying no difficult in ministry?
5. Will the majority of our people understand our ministry process *before* focus takes place, *as* focus is taking place, or *after* focus has occurred?
6. As a steward of people's time and money, what is God speaking to me about?

NINE

Becoming Simple

Just Do It.
~ NIKE

Clarity ➤ Movement ➤ Alignment ➤ Focus

There is a scene in *Super-Size Me* that is disturbing. We are not talking about the one where Morgan Spurlock, the producer, vomits on the ground. OK, that is disturbing as well. But we are referring to a different scene.

In this scene Morgan Spurlock is seeking to prove how effectively McDonalds impacts upcoming generations. So he meets with schoolchildren and shows them pictures of famous people. Most of the children recognize a depiction of George Washington. All recognize a depiction of Ronald McDonald. None of them recognize a common depiction of Jesus Christ.

None. Not one.

Yes, we know the depiction is probably inaccurate, but you get the point. Most children in America are growing up without any knowledge of Jesus. We are living in a post-Christian culture. For upcoming generations Christ is no longer the starting point. Children and teenagers no longer rebel against the standard. Today there is no standard.

Nearly ten years ago Thom predicted this would be the case. In his book *The Bridger Generation*, he presented research that indicated only 4 percent of upcoming generations would become Christians. Sadly we are living in the reality of that prediction.[1]

McDonalds is influencing future generations. Churches are not.

While the impact of McDonalds is spreading, the impact of the church is shrinking. In fact, most churches are spiritually stagnant and declining numerically. And this decline is in the midst of an increasing population.

The church, as a whole, is doing more and more. And the church, as a whole, is making less and less of a difference.

Church complexity is costly. The cost is beyond time and money. The kingdom is not expanding. Lives are not being changed. Transformation is not happening. Churches are not growing.

Moving to simple needs to happen. For the sake of the kingdom, the church, and the people you serve, it is time for action. In many churches, there has been too much talk. New statements mask the same behavior and the same paradigms. New strategies cover up the complexity. In most churches, nothing really changes.

The kingdom is not about chatter. It is about action. Nike has some great theology. It is time to just do it. It is time to refuse to be a programmer. It is time to design and implement a simple process that moves people toward spiritual transformation.

It is time for change. The alternative is to continue leading dying churches filled with spiritually anemic people.

Change or die. Those are the choices.

Change or Die

A recent medical study reveals just how difficult change is for people. Roughly 600,000 people have heart bypasses a year in America. These people are told after their bypasses that they must change their lifestyle. The heart bypass is a temporary fix. They must change their diet. They must quit smoking and drinking. They must exercise and reduce stress.

In essence, the doctors say, "Change or die."

You would think that a near-death experience would forever grab the attention of the patients. You would think they would vote for change. You would think the argument for change is so compelling that the patients would make the appropriate lifestyle alterations. Sadly that is not the case.

Ninety percent of the heart patients do not change. They remain the same, living the status quo. Study after study indicates that two years after heart surgery, the patients have not altered their behavior. Instead of making changes for life, they choose death.[2]

Change is that difficult. The majority of heart patients choose not to change. They act as if they would rather die. In the same way the majority of churches choose not to change. They would rather die. Tragically, in most churches, the pain of change is greater than the pain of ineffectiveness.

While moving to a simple church approach needs to happen, the transition will not be easy. It is change. Becoming a simple church is difficult. In fact, the longer your church has been complex, the more difficult the transition will be.

Attention church planters: this information is good news for you. While you have little money, own no land or buildings, you are able to design from scratch.

Cluttered church leaders do not have that luxury. Ceasing to be a pack rat will be extremely challenging. Moving out the clutter will be more painful than a garage sale. Leadership expert Tom Peters once commented, "It is easier to kill an organization than it is to change it."[3]

Please do not take the easy route. Do not kill your church. You have seen that happen. It is horrible. Do not treat moving toward simple as a corporate restructuring or downsizing initiative. The church is the body of believers, filled with real people.

There is a tension here, isn't there?

On one hand, you must move to simple as fast as you can. So much depends on it. The longer you are complex, the longer your focus is divided. If you remain complex, your process for transformation remains unclear. The longer you are complex, the longer your church is congested. People remain unchanged. And this bothers you. It should.

On the other hand, you must move to simple slowly. You have the heart of a shepherd, and you care for the people in your church. Becoming simple will be painful for some people. They cannot imagine losing some of the traditions and programs.

So this tension exists. You desire to see changes happen now for the sake of the kingdom and the unchanged people in your community. Yet you desire to bring the people you already have along with you. How is this tension resolved?

Change theorists argue over this tension. Some advocate that change should happen all at once. Quickly. These people insist that it is less painful to cut off your arm with one fell swoop as opposed to one section at a time. They advise to tie all changes to an overarching vision and go for it. They believe that big sweeping changes produce results quickly, which ultimately validates the change.

Other change theorists shake their heads in disagreement to this advice. They believe change should be incremental, slow, and methodical. These people insist the goal of change is not destruction but transformation. They believe that by implementing change slowly, people are given an opportunity to adapt and grow. They propose that incremental change is wise because each change builds a culture where more change can occur.

Which group is right? Both approaches to change have succeeded. Both approaches to change have failed. You must live with this tension. Now/later. Fast/slow. Sweeping/incremental change.

Good news. You have the Holy Spirit. Pray for discernment. Allow God to give you wisdom and grant you favor. Get on God's timetable. Move to simple as God leads. Use wisdom and compassion in becoming a simple church.

Here is the bottom line: Get there as fast as you can but not faster.

Back to Pastor Rush

It has been three months since Pastor Rush had the sacred and scary moment in his office. The moment was bittersweet. It was sweet because he sensed a new direction. It was bitter because he knew change would be imminent.

It was the moment where he stared at a plethora of church models on his shelf and realized everything was mixed together like a spiritual bowl of leftover casserole. He realized, in the midst of the busyness, that his church did not have a clear *how*. At the church Pastor Rush serves, there is not a process in place to move people to spiritual maturity.

His moment was soon interrupted. Phone calls and preparation pulled him away. But the unrest has continued. Over the last few months, Pastor Rush has seriously evaluated his church for the first time in years. He has walked around. He has looked. He has asked questions.

As Pastor Rush walked around, he realized things were done poorly. While activity abounds, excellence is missing. There is so much happening, so much to manage, so many programs to produce. Attention, energy, resources, and people are divided.

Complexity is often synonymous with mediocrity.

In his personal devotions Pastor Rush has been reading through the latter half of the Old Testament. It has been years since he has read and studied the Minor Prophets, the little books before the New Testament begins. God used the first chapter in the book of Malachi to confirm that change is not an option. Pastor Rush has been wrestling with Malachi 1. Each time he reads it, he sees himself and other people in his church. His heart is filled with conviction.

Malachi 1

In Malachi 1, God confronts the leaders, the priests. The priests were offering leftover sacrifices to God. No one really likes leftovers. Neither does God.

> "A son honors his father, and a servant his master.
> But if I am a father, where is My honor? And if I am
> a master, where is your fear of Me? says the LORD of
> Hosts to you priests, who despise My name."

Yet you ask: "How have we despised Your name?"
"By presenting defiled food on My altar."
You ask: "How have we defiled You?"
When you say: "The LORD's table is contemptible."
"When you present a blind animal for sacrifice, is
it not wrong? And when you present a lame or sick
[animal], is it not wrong? Bring it to your governor!
Would he be pleased with you or show you favor?" asks
the LORD of Hosts. "And now ask for God's favor. Will
He be gracious to us? Since this has come from your
hands, will He show any of you favor?" asks the LORD
of Hosts. "I wish one of you would shut the temple
doors, so you would no longer kindle a useless fire on
My altar! I am not pleased with you," says the LORD of
Hosts, "and I will accept no offering from your hands.

"For My name will be great among the nations,
from the rising of the sun to its setting. Incense and
pure offerings will be presented in My name in every
place because My name will be great among the
nations," says the LORD of Hosts.

But you are profaning it when you say: "The Lord's
table is defiled, and its product, its food, is contemptible." You also say: "Look, what a nuisance!" "And you
scorn it," says the LORD of Hosts. "You bring stolen,
lame, or sick animals. You bring this as an offering!
Am I to accept that from your hands?" asks the LORD.

"The deceiver is cursed who has an acceptable male
in his flock and makes a vow but sacrifices a defective
animal to the Lord. For I am a great King," says the
LORD of Hosts, "and My name will be feared among
the nations." (Mal. 1:6–14)

The priests had specific instructions for what type of sacrifices they were to offer to God. According to Leviticus 22, they were to bring only pure and unblemished animals to sacrifice. They were to bring God the best.

Yet the priests were responding to God, their Master and Father, by offering the worst animals. This is an unacceptable offering to God. He reminds them who He is. Seven times in the passage, God refers to Himself as the LORD of Hosts, the Lord Almighty. He deserves, desires, and demands the best.

These people forgot that. They actually had the audacity to offer to God blind and diseased animals. God tells the priests to try offering those kinds of sacrifices to the governor.

God even tells the priests to shut down the temple, to shut the doors to cancel services, to just stop everything. God has never been impressed with halfhearted worship. The mediocrity is sickening to God.

He tells the priests that He will accept no offering from their hands. In essence God says, "If I cannot have the best of you, the best from you, then please do not bring anything to me." According to God's system, something is not better than nothing.

The people in Malachi stayed busy. They continued to go through the motions of serving God. They kept having church week after week with no intensity or intentionality. They were checking off their to-do list.

Remember, these were the priests. The priests did not call the people to a higher standard. In their minds everything was fine as long as sacrifices were offered. As long as they fulfilled the *what*, everything was OK.

God was concerned about the *how*. It mattered to God deeply *how* sacrifices were offered to Him. It mattered to God deeply *how* the priests served Him. These priests created a culture of mediocrity. And this profaned the name of God.

Mediocrity bothers God because it violates His nature and behavior. God is an excellent God. His character is flawless. Excellence flows from the nature of who God is. Everything God has ever done has been excellent. Creation, the sunset, the ocean, and His resurrection point to His excellent nature.

The leaders offered an inappropriate response to God. Instead of reflecting His attribute of excellence to the world, they modeled mediocrity. God was frustrated with the leaders because they set the pace and the tone. The people took their cues from them. If the priests offered second best to God, the people would as well.

Multiple issues have converged at once in Pastor Rush's mind. People are not being transformed in his church because there is not a simple process. Everything is too complex, too cluttered. And this clutter fosters mediocrity. It is impossible to offer excellence when focus is so divided. Seemingly people continue to go through the motions while no one is ever changed.

Most importantly, Pastor Rush feels that God is not pleased. He and his staff are running mediocre programs instead of making disciples. Pastor Rush has decided that change must happen. Or he will die, internally. The pain of mediocrity and ineffectiveness has become too great.

As the leader, he knows the change needs to begin with him.

Perhaps you are where Pastor Rush is. You do not want to spend the rest of your life leading mediocre programs. You do not want to go through the motions of ministry without a clear process for transformation. Perhaps the clutter and the complexity are unbearable. Your calling from God remains unchanged. It keeps you going, but you know there is a better way to do ministry.

You are not alone.

Hundreds of church leaders have shared with us the same frustration. That is the reason for this book. We pray it has given you a framework for a simple ministry process.

We conclude with four steps to becoming a simple church. These steps summarize much of the book and frame the transition for you.

For some these steps will take several months. For others these steps will take several years. Remember, the longer your church has been complex, the harder the transition will be.

Step 1: Design a Simple Process (Clarity)

You must first design a simple ministry process for your church—on paper. This design is not about changing any programs or structures. Not yet. During this step, you are simply exploring what a process for discipleship would look like at your church. The process must first be in your head and heart before it becomes a reality.

Use this step to create an environment receptive to change. Let people know that a process is not in place, that disciples are not intentionally made. Share that presently discipleship, if it happens, just kind of happens by accident. The conversation may be uncomfortable if you have been a leader there for a long time, but you must create some dissatisfaction if people are going to be open to change.

Do not make the mistake of beginning with your existing programs. Begin with a blank sheet of paper. Do not try to squeeze the process into your programs. Allow the simple process that God gives you to be your starting point.

Invest a significant amount of time in the Scriptures and in prayer. Read about discipleship. Allow God to breathe into you *what* a disciple at your church should look like. Involve others in the discussion. Meet with spiritually mature staff and key leaders and have open discussions about what kind of disciples God is calling you to make.

Once you have had these times with God and others, narrow your definition of discipleship down to a few key points. After you have invested the appropriate amount of time, you should be able to fill in the blanks to the following statement. Disciples at our church are: _____, _____, _____, and _____.

You may have fewer blanks, or you may have more. However, less is best. The more blanks you have, the longer your process will be.

At this point there is no reason to get nervous. You have not implemented any changes. You still have not cut any programs or events. You are simply discussing *what* discipleship looks like.

Now it is time to discuss *how* it happens.

After you have chosen a few key aspects of discipleship, place them in sequential order. Discuss with others *how* people progress through the aspects of discipleship you have listed. Talk about *how* spiritual transformation takes place. Share *how* spiritual growth has happened in your life and the lives of others you know. The process must be personal.

Place your aspects of discipleship in order based on differing levels of commitment. Remember, the process must be clearly defined. There must be a starting point and a next step. The first step in the process should be the first level of commitment.

Describe your definition of discipleship in process terms. At this point you should be able to fill in the blanks to the following statement: People become mature disciples at our church by

_____   _____

_____   _____

The number of terms and the terms themselves in this set of blanks should be the same as the previous set. Now they are in sequential order.

Spend time discussing and preaching your process. The clearer this process for spiritual transformation is to people in your church, the easier the next transition steps will be.

Step 2: Place Your Key Programs Along the Process (Movement)

After you have designed a process on paper, it is time to implement it. It is one thing to have a simple process written down, it is entirely another thing to place the programs along the process. This point is where the transition gets more difficult. In fact, each upcoming step will be more challenging.

Choose one churchwide program for each phase of your simple process. The purpose of the program should coincide with that particular part of the process. You may have some programs left over, meaning they do not fit into your process. At this point the complexity becomes obvious. Do not feel that you have to eliminate those programs right away. Take your time and move through the transition as God leads. Elimination is part of the last step.

At this point you still have not gotten rid of anything. However, you may have to change the focus of some of your programs. You will want to be sure each program in your process is designed to meet that specific aspect of discipleship effectively. Here is where the resistance to change happens. When you tweak a program, you are tweaking tradition.

The first program is the entry point into your process. The following programs should require greater levels of commitment. Remember, you want to progress people to greater levels of spiritual vitality. You want to be able to move people through the simple process.

After you have finished this step, you should be able to fill in the following blanks.

_____(program)   _____(program)
_____(program)   _____(program)

Step 3: Unite All Ministries Around the Process (Alignment)

After you have followed steps 1 and 2, you will have a simple process with programs strategically placed. Now you must align each ministry around the same process. If each age-specific ministry uses the same words to describe the process, the people in the church will grasp it much faster.

The more you involve other leaders in the design of the simple process, the easier it will be to unite them around it. If they are in the discussions, you are simply challenging everyone to put into practice what is agreed upon.

When new leaders are hired or recruited, be sure they believe wholeheartedly in your simple process. As new ministries begin, ensure they understand how they fit into the overall picture.

Step 4: Begin to Eliminate Things Outside the Process (Focus)

OK, this is where the change is REALLY felt. Please notice, that here is the only time in the entire book we used all caps to emphasize a point.

Most people will be grateful that a process for discipleship is developed in your church. Most people will appreciate that the programs are purposeful, that they are a part of a bigger picture. And most people will enjoy the unity of all ministries moving in the same direction. Things in your church will be clearer and more focused. Remember that people do appreciate simplicity.

However, some people will struggle with abandoning other programs to focus solely on the ministry process God has given your church. Some of the programs will have deep traditions and rich history. You must use wisdom in step 4.

If you consistently discuss the simple process and the programs used to move people through the process, some people will begin to wonder how additional programs fit. You will even begin to have people ask you that question. It is an awkward moment, but a great opportunity for discussion.

In time it is important that you eliminate programs and events that do not fit. They are a distraction from the process, and they prohibit your church from enjoying all the benefits of a simple church.

To be a simple church, you must implement a process that is clear and moves people. You must insist that all ministries align to the process, and you must refuse to allow it to become cluttered. You must stay focused.

While becoming simple will be difficult, it is also worth it. The gates of hell will be pushed back, dented, and damaged. The upcoming generations will be exposed to the gospel and goodness of our God. And the people in your church will be placed in the pathway of God's transforming power.

Simple. It is so compelling.

The simple church revolution has begun.

Are you in?

GROUP DISCUSSION QUESTIONS

1. What is the relationship between complexity and mediocrity?
2. How complex are we?
3. How receptive to change are our leaders?
4. How receptive to change is our entire church?
5. How long do you think each transition step would take at our church?

The Postscript (or what we have learned)

Five years have passed since the initial release of *Simple Church* and to say that we are overwhelmed with the response would be a vast understatement. And our shock with the response is not a statement of humility (unfortunately), but the reality of the nature of the book. Let's be honest—the book you are holding is a nerdy research project. The research was extensive and the results were very noteworthy; therefore, a book followed. But research books don't tend to make anyone's "favorite books" list. Typically, normal people don't read church research books on vacation.

We do. But we are not normal.

If you are reading this on vacation—welcome to the club.

Not only is the book a research-based book, but it is also loaded with "insider language." Meaning we wrote the book for pastors and church leaders. The book is filled with the kinds of conversations we have during consultations, during staff meetings, and during strategy sessions with church leaders. We never thought regular godly church people would read the book or have the book given to them from a pastor in their church.

If you are one of those people, we apologize. If we knew you would be reading this book when we wrote it, we would have been more cognizant of our insider language. Eric serves as executive pastor of Christ Fellowship in Miami. Never has his church heard discussion about "horizontal measurement," "strategic movement," or "programming along your discipleship process." These are organizational concepts the leadership wrestles with, but they have never been preached or woven into a message.

Despite the research nature and the insider lingo, God has chosen to use the book to challenge thousands of church leaders. We have heard incredible stories of transformation and gospel growth from church plants to existing churches that were a bit too cluttered and un-focused. We are deeply honored God used us to encourage leaders to evaluate their discipleship process—honored to know that churches have been helped in small or big ways. Augustine reminds us "all truth is God's truth." We believe that the strength of the book is based on truth: secondarily, truth discovered through the research (a form of God's general revelation), and primarily, truth revealed in Scripture (God's special revelation).

At the same time, the book is far from perfect. It is definitely not infallible or inerrant. It is incomplete and not comprehensive. We simply reported on what we discovered in the research. Now after five years of discussions and observations with church leaders, we humbly submit the postscript. Here are the six most significant lessons learned related to *Simple Church* in the last five years.

Churches Drift

In early 2008, Howard Schultz, the CEO of Starbucks noticed a significant drift in his company. While vacationing in Europe, Schultz observed the passion of baristas in local coffee shops. It was as if each barista was pouring his heart and soul into the coffee. Brewing coffee appeared to be an art form. But in his beloved Starbucks, Schultz recalled the feeling that baristas were simply going through the motions.

Perhaps the problem was not with the baristas. Perhaps the company as a whole had drifted.

In the formative years of Starbucks, the attention of the baristas was on the coffee. But with the emergence of other food items and music, their attention became divided; the quality of the coffee and the customer experience spiraled downward. The company drifted. So Schultz called a "time-out." Starbucks needed to return to the essence of Starbucks, to their core mission.

To address the drift, Schultz decided to shut down Starbucks in the United States for several hours. So on a regular afternoon in February 2008, approximately 7,000 Starbucks were closed for three hours. And during those three hours, approximately 135,000 employees were re-trained on the original essence of the company—making coffee.

Churches drift too.

We drift away from the core message of the Christian faith, the gospel. We move away from the essence of the Christian faith, the good news that our holy God rescued us from our sins by placing Himself on a cross in our place to secure our salvation. We drift away from the core mission of the church: making disciples. We add so many extras to the essence of who we are. We drift.

Drift is always bad. You don't drift into physical fitness or spiritual growth. And churches do not drift into spiritual health or kingdom advancement. We drift away from those things, not toward them.

And drift never corrects itself.

Perhaps you have noticed a drift in your vehicle. Instead of driving with your hands centered on the wheel, you drive with your hands on one side of the wheel because the car keeps pulling off the road. Over time the drift has crept into your vehicle. You know you need to address the issue. But it is easier to just cope with it. In the same way, many churches merely cope with the drift that is plaguing them.

In relation to *Simple Church*, we have noticed two common drifts in churches. The two drifts are related; if the first drift is occurring in your church, the second is present as well.

First, **we drift toward complexity**. During the research behind *Simple Church* and in many subsequent consultations, church leaders have confessed, "I feel like a program manager. God pulled me into ministry because I wanted to see people transformed into the image of Christ, because I wanted to serve His church, because He gave me a passion to make disciples. But now, I just manage programs."

Many pastors have confessed that success for them is managing programs better than the person who led the ministry before them. Some feel as if they went to the church they serve and were handed a slate of programs by whomever hired them. The implicit expectation being, "Your role is to do those programs better than they were done before you arrived."

We have met with staff teams that spend hours in meetings every week managing the church calendar. Some churches confess they feel guilty if something is not on the calendar. If there are several empty days on the calendar, they believe something must be added. The calendar, in some settings, justifies the existence of the church and of her leaders.

We drift toward religious complexity. Martin Luther said, "Religion is the deep default of the human heart." We always drift toward religion.

In the gospels, we see the drift of religious complexity occur with the Pharisees. The Pharisees were a group of people who sincerely believed they were living to please God. The word "Pharisee" literally means "separated ones." So in all likelihood, many of the Pharisees began with good intentions. They wanted to please God, to live a life that was separate from unrighteousness and impurity.

So they developed complicated lists that would regulate their own righteousness. They took the core commands of God and added their own rules and regulations to them. For example, they took the command to "remember the Sabbath and keep it holy" and placed thousands of minute laws on top of the command. If you were a Jew during the time the Pharisees were perceived as the experts in the Law, you would have found the Sabbath much more stressful than your work week.

The rules the Pharisees placed on people were completely overwhelming. For example, baths could not be taken because water might spill on the floor. And if the water were wiped up, the perpetrator would be guilty of working on the Sabbath because he would have cleaned his floor. A woman would not be allowed to look in the mirror on the Sabbath because if she looked in the mirror, she may see a gray hair and be tempted to pull it out which would constitute work and be a violation of the Sabbath. False teeth could not be worn on the Sabbath because they weighed enough to be considered a burden too heavy to be carried on the Sabbath.

When the Pharisees attempted to pull Jesus into the discussion about the rules and regulations He told them simply:

"Love the Lord your God with all your heart, with all your soul, and with all your mind. This is the greatest and most important commandment. The second is

like it: Love your neighbor as yourself. All the Law and
the Prophets depend on these two commandments."
(Matt. 22:37–40 HCSB)
Jesus addressed the drift.

Sadly, most churches choose to cope with the drift instead
of addressing it. Churches cope with the drift toward complexity in the same way individuals cope with complexity.

To cope with complexity, some choose to multi-task. There
is "so much to do," so people attempt to do multiple things at
the same time. Many Americans text while in traffic, check
Twitter while in lines, and talk on the cell phone while riding a
bike at the gym. People even brag about their ability to multi-task, their ability to handle many obligations and juggle many
balls. People often advocate that multi-tasking makes them
more effective, but research says the opposite.

Research shows that when you receive frequent interruptions while working on a task, your performance drops the
equivalent of ten IQ points. In other words, when you multi-task you are ten points dumber on the core task than you are
if you just focused on the core task. Some of us cannot afford
to multi-task.[1]

Compare the effects of multi-tasking to smoking weed.
Smoking pot drops your performance the equivalent of four
IQ points. We are not suggesting you smoke weed. We are suggesting you realize the adverse implications of multi-tasking.

Churches are notorious for multi-tasking. It is how they
cope with complexity.

Many move in a myriad of directions never realizing the full
potential of a team rallying around a singular mission. Many
jump from new initiative to new initiative or new vision to new
vision before any of them actually takes root in the life of the
church. Many churches attempt an overabundance of activities,

events, and programs. Thus they offer them all with mediocrity as their energy and resources are spread thinly and evenly
across a massive menu of "stuff."

If your church is multi-tasking, you are merely coping with
the drift toward complexity. Another coping mechanism in
cluttered and complicated churches is outsourcing.

In our personal lives, we deal with complexity and busyness
by outsourcing tasks to others. Some things are appropriate
to outsource. If the week is busy in the middle of the summer,
it is completely appropriate to outsource lawn care to someone else so you have more time for what is essential in your
life. But there are some things we should never outsource.
A parent should never outsource raising children to someone else. A husband should never outsource dating his wife
to another person. For those of us married with children,
father/mother and husband/wife are essential aspects of who
we are.

We are not concerned with churches outsourcing web
design, custodial services, or graphic design. Churches may
choose to outsource important tasks that are not essential to
their character and calling. However, there are some tasks a
church must never outsource because these tasks are embedded into what Jesus envisions a church being and doing.

Sadly, because many churches drift toward complexity,
many churches have outsourced the mission of God. They let
others handle mission. They tout how much they give to a mission agency as their commitment to missions. They place pictures of missionaries on their bulletin boards and boldly declare
their mission mind-set. We applaud missions giving and missionaries on bulletin boards. But these expressions must not be
all a church does for those outside of herself. If mission giving
is the totality of the church's mission engagement, the church

has outsourced mission to those they pay to do it in order for their mission's conscience to be satisfied.

If a church is multi-tasking or out-sourcing mission, this typically indicates the church has drifted toward complexity. We drift toward complex chaos. We drift toward entropy. Even after establishing a simple process for discipleship, churches are constantly tempted to drift toward complexity.

Drifting toward complexity is easy. Staying simple requires great discipline.

Second, *we drift off mission*. If a church is complicated, she will not have the energy or the resources available to be highly engaged in mission. The church will spend her time existing for herself, setting up systems for herself, and communicating to herself.

In a recent consultation with a church in a slow decline, our brief analysis revealed that 92 percent of their annual budget was allotted to debt retirement and compensation. In other words, it took 92 percent of their resources just to pull off the system of church. That particular church has little left to offer the world and community surrounding her.

Jesus shared a story with His disciples illustrating that we must not drift off mission, that churches must exist for people beyond us.

> He presented another parable to them: "The kingdom of heaven is like a mustard seed that a man took and sowed in his field. It's the smallest of all the seeds, but when grown, it's taller than the vegetables and becomes a tree, so that the birds of the sky come and nest in its branches." (Matt. 13:31–32)

Jesus' disciples were wondering if His kingdom was really going anywhere. Jesus points out that His Kingdom would have a small start, just as a mustard seed starts small. From a human perspective, His arrival on this earth was a minor and unnoticed event to the vast majority of humanity. He was born in a barn and placed in a manger. After His birth, He grew up far from the influence and affluence of the Roman Empire. One would say, "Nazareth, can anything good come from Nazareth?" (John 1:46) He invited 12 disciples to live with him and follow him. These 12 disciples were according to the religious crowd, unschooled ordinary men (Acts 4:13). After Jesus died, rose from the dead, and ascended back to heaven, about 120 people gathered together in prayer in Jerusalem waiting for direction from the Holy Spirit on what to do next. The kingdom of God started very small.

But it did not stay small. "It is the largest of garden plants and became a tree." This weekend, millions of people throughout the world will gather to worship Christ because of what He has done in our lives. Some will worship in church buildings. Others will worship in schools, theaters, or homes. Some will worship in secret hiding places because it is illegal to be Christian in their country. We will worship in different languages and with different styles and cultural values, but we will worship the same Jesus and study the same Holy Scripture.

The passage is beautiful. What Jesus declared would happen has been fulfilled. The kingdom is now a large plant, a tree. But the passage does not end here. Jesus told His disciples that as the kingdom of God would grow, something amazing would happen—"the birds of the air come and perch in its branches."

The phrase "so that the birds of the air come and perch in its branches" took the disciples back to several Old Testament passages describing earthly kingdoms that were so powerful and fruitful that people outside of those kingdoms benefited from them. Jesus was speaking about His kingdom, so the disciples would have made the connection to earthly kingdoms they studied in the Old Testament. The disciples knew the story of the Assyrian kingdom, a kingdom that at one time was so strong that other nations were impacted and influenced by the Assyrians, a kingdom where all "the birds of the air nested in its branches" (Ezek. 31:6).

The disciples also knew the story of the Babylonian kingdom. In Daniel 4, Nebuchadnezzar has a dream where he sees a tall tree standing. In the dream, the tree grew and was strong and large enough that everyone in the whole earth could see the tree. There were tons of fruit on the tree, enough for everyone to eat. *"And the birds of the air lived in its branches"* (Dan. 4:12). Nebuchadnezzar asked Daniel to interpret his dream. Daniel tells the king of Babylon, "You are that tree" (Dan. 4:22). Daniel was essentially telling Nebuchadnezzar, "Your kingdom, the Babylonian kingdom, is so fruitful and is so influential that others are impacted by your influence. Nations are finding comfort, security, and food in the tree that is your kingdom."

The vision Jesus articulated to His disciples is that the kingdom of God will be such an influential and powerful movement in the culture that those outside the kingdom of God will benefit from the influence of the kingdom of God. People will benefit from the kingdom's existence and they will come and rest and receive shelter in its branches. The kingdom of God will be such an influential force that the community, the city, and the culture will benefit from the presence of the kingdom of God expressed in our churches.

God's desire for His church is that our faith will transform not only us, but also those around us. His desire is that the cities, the communities, and the neighborhoods where our churches are planted will benefit from our faith regardless if they believe what we believe, profess the faith we profess, or live by the values of our kingdom.

We drift toward complexity. We drift away from mission. The two are related. When you are complex, you tend to be inward. There is so much to manage at the church building; there is little time to think strategically about the community. There is minimal energy to serve those in the community. At the same time, when you drift off mission you will naturally become complex and complicated. Something will dominate your time if the mission of God does not dominate your heart.

Thinking Process is a Mammoth Shift

We never intended for *Simple Church* to be considered a church model. Notice that the first sentence in the first chapter reads, "This is not a church model." There are so many unaddressed issues (intentionally so) that prevent the book from being a comprehensive church model. We do not discuss issues that are critical in a church model: music style, teaching style, dress, type of sermon, or church architecture. We do not advocate a specific church polity: pastor-led, elder-led, or even unbiblically deacon-led. While we have convictions on all the aforementioned, they were not researched thus preventing us from commenting on them in a research-based book. Furthermore, we are not comfortable or capable of suggesting an all-encompassing church model.

The proclivity of leaders to look for another church model is a sign of the church's shallowness and not its maturity.

We get nervous when someone speaks of his or her church becoming a "simple church" because the phrase sounds like a new church model, which we never advocated. Eric serves as executive pastor of Christ Fellowship in Miami. Since the writing of the book, by God's grace, the church has grown by several thousand people. But Eric never refers to the church he serves as a "simple church." Yes, there is a simple process for discipleship that guides all the church does, but the leaders speak of their vision and mission of "connecting people to God, others, ministry, and the world" not being a "simple church." The majority of the people in the church have no idea Eric coauthored the book.

In the book we advocate designing a process for discipleship. Therefore, the overarching key word in the book is "process" not "simple." Here is a confession: the original title of the book was "Process Centered Ministry," but many friends told us that it was a horrifically boring title and that only nerdy research people would read a book with that title while on vacation.

We are glad we listened. Kind of.

We say "kind of" because unfortunately some leaders literally read an entire book built on the premise of a discipleship process and walked away with agendas other than that of a discipleship process. Based on our research and based on Scripture, we are convinced that all churches, regardless of the model they choose, should have a process for making disciples. If a church is not clear on their discipleship process, people will move in a multitude of directions. Process is essential.

The book is fundamentally not about a new statement, even a "process statement." We are not suggesting that what is lacking in any church is a new statement. We are advocating designing a process for discipleship.

Admittedly, the word "process" is less captivating than "vision" or "mission" but the concept is absolutely critical. And we have learned that to challenge leaders to think in terms of "process" is a mammoth shift.

During the Great Awakening, there were two famous preachers: George Whitefield and John Wesley. Most would say that Whitefield was the superior orator. He was known as the phenomenal communicator of his day. Some, particularly those from our theological tradition, would say he preached a more biblically accurate message. But years later as historians would compare the impact of Whitefield's ministry to Wesley's, they discovered Wesley was much more effective.

Whitefield showed up and preached. He did so, well and faithfully. But his ministry was confined to the preaching of the Word, which we firmly believe is absolutely essential. Wesley, though, was committed to more than just the event where he would proclaim the message. He worked hard on developing a process that moved people to classes, organized people in groups, and then challenged them to engage the world. Wesley did not *just* preach. He cared about what happened after; he cared about implementing a discipleship process.

Wesley understood process. It is called Methodism.

The entire *Simple Church* book unpacked how to design a process that is clear, moves people through stages of spiritual growth, creates unity, and is focused. But here are some recent observations related to designing a process in your church.

View discipleship as the whole process. People have often asked, "Where does discipleship fit into the process?" The question reveals a faulty definition of discipleship because the question is typically about curriculum or learning environments. We have often equated discipleship with information. Discipleship is not about information. It is about transformation. The end result of discipleship is not knowledge but obedience. Jesus said, "Go and make disciples, teaching them to obey everything." Not just teaching them everything. When you design a process for discipleship, view discipleship as the whole process.

Be careful not to over-program early in your discipleship process. A mistake we have seen played out multiple times is when church leaders craft (or borrow) a new vision or mission statement and quickly throw all their existing programs under the new statement. The old just gets baptized with new nomenclature.

Sprinkling the old with new lingo was a very common response to "purpose-driven church." Though Rick Warren articulates process throughout the book, many people only walked away with five words: worship, discipleship, ministry, evangelism, and fellowship. Many leaders threw the five words up on a board, and re-categorized all their existing programs and triumphantly claimed to be "purpose-driven."

And as long as someone (a staff or lay leader) could articulate some event or program as meeting one of those five words, the event or program made the sacred calendar. There was a secret to the purpose-driven programming dilemma. If you were not sure what purpose your idea met, you could attach the "fellowship" tag to your idea because anything could be fellowship.

With *Simple Church*, some have done the same thing. Church leaders find a new statement and dump all their existing programs into the new statement. It is painful to observe after we wrote the book proclaiming the need to program minimally around a discipleship process. The problem with the re-categorization approach is that if leaders just place everything they are doing under a new phrase, they have not really designed a process for spiritual transformation. They have merely re-organized programs.

A major consequence embedded in haphazard re-categorization is that church leaders will unintentionally hold people early in the articulated discipleship process. Because people only have so much time, over-programming early in a discipleship process prevents people from moving to steps placed deeper in the process.

For example, imagine XYZ church articulates that in their discipleship process they desire to move people from large worship environments to places of biblical community to places of mission engagement. Perhaps they say, "Our vision is to exalt, encourage, and engage." But XYZ church merely re-categorizes all their programming under their new statement. They place Sunday morning worship services and Sunday night worship services under "exalt." Under "encourage," they place Sunday school, discipleship groups, home prayer groups, men's ministry, women's ministry, and a plethora of other things. Each week in their worship services, the leaders compete for time to promote their "encourage" programs.

Do you see the problem? If someone were to actually go to all of the programs promoted, the individual would be at six different things each week. And he or she still has not served nor engaged unbelievers outside the church. Over-programming early in your process competes with your process. Over-programming hampers the body by complicating the lives of church members to the point that there is no margin for service or mission.

Don't program against your church vision. Your programs should be in harmony with your vision.

Mission must be deeply embedded in your process. We are concerned that some church processes end with the church. In other words, the end result of some discipleship processes in the church is the church itself. We believe that mission must be deeply embedded in a discipleship process that is truly reflective of the type of disciples Jesus makes. If your discipleship process sounds like, "Come to our church, get connected, and help us do church better," you need to repent of too shallow a vision for discipleship. Surely the end result of discipleship is not your church merely doing church better.

Live your process. Since the release of the book, many church staff teams have articulated that they want to move people from worship services to small groups or Sunday School. Yet, often, when we ask the leadership team how many of them are in a group or class, the typical response is less than half. If leaders do not live the vision they are articulating, the vision has a faint chance of being realized.

John Kotter of Harvard Business School wrote, "Behavior from important people in the organization that is contrary to the vision overwhelms all other forms of communication."[2] In other words, if the leaders do not live what they are asking the people to live, time was wasted on the new logo, money was squandered on the new banner, and the statement in the bulletin is worthless. Pastor, here is a good test if your church is too complicated: "Can you do all you are asking your people to do?"

While the first two learnings are very general, the next three are related to specific issues and opportunities facing churches in our current generation.

Simple Is Reproducible

Regardless of your position on churches having multiple campuses, the data points to "the multi-site church movement" as being a sustainable paradigm for the foreseeable future. There are more and more churches entering the world of multiple campuses. And once a church goes multi-site, the entire fabric of the church is altered. In other words, multi-site changes the whole church to the point that it is unlikely churches will teeter back and forth from being multi-site to mono-site. Thus, "multi-site church" is a new and increasing reality in the church world.

When a pastor asks if his church should consider launching another campus, there are two essential questions that must be answered. (1) *Is your church healthy?* The question is about health, not perfection. A church must be healthy before reproduction occurs because churches reproduce what they are. (2) *Is your church reproducible?* If the second campus is going to truly be the same church only in a different location, then the church strategy and programming must be reproducible.

Some complex churches have moved into multiple locations and the following scenario has occurred. The new campus does not offer all the programming the original campus offers. Some love the simplicity of the new campus. They are drawn to the entrepreneurial spirit and streamlined approach. However, others who know the church for its menu of programs continually struggle that the new campus does not offer them all the programming the original campus does. Tension threatens to become disunity. At best, wise and strong leaders are able to navigate the tension. But the two campuses do not feel like the same church. Only the message and the name are the same. The vision, the philosophy, and the approach feel very different.

Our casual observation is that the churches that are able to quickly move to multiple campuses have a simple and clear vision with minimal and reproducible programming. Since the release of *Simple Church,* the church Eric serves has moved from one campus to five campuses. Christ Fellowship was not prepared to move into multiple campuses across Miami until there was first a clear and simple discipleship process that would guide programming that could be reproduced.

Five Guys Burgers and Fries has reproduced very rapidly in recent years. In 2003, *Five Guys* existed exclusively in five locations in the DC Metro area. Since 2003, the franchise has launched over 620 new locations.

They are reproducible because they are simple. *Five Guys* only does a few things (burgers, fries, and hotdogs) and they do what they do very well. Here is an excerpt from their Web site.

> **Q:** Does *Five Guys* plan to add any menu items (i.e., milkshakes, chili, etc.)?
>
> **A:** *Five Guys* does not currently have plans to add any items to our menu. We follow the philosophy of focusing on a few items, and serving them to the best of our ability.

Five Guys has a wise strategy for reproduction. Simple is reproducible. Complex is not.

Simple Requires Aligned Staffing

There is much talk in the American church world about the right kind of church staffing. Of course, we understand that the majority of churches only have one paid staff member: the pastor. Some of these churches have volunteer or nominally paid staff members.

We heard from many church leaders that their staff alignment did not fit within the simple concept. These leaders told us that they were staffing according to church programs: youth programs; children's programs; education programs; and others. How could they become a simple church when they were clearly staffed to be a program church?

Some of the church leaders told us that they actually changed the staff position names to reflect more accurately the components of the discipleship process. In essence, the staff names were directly tied to the mission statement of the church

Still other leaders shared with us that they made some modifications in position titles, but they focused more on the content of the position description than the name itself.

Both are good examples of churches aligning their staff with the process of discipleship inherent in a simple church. The overarching issue is that every staff member must be philosophically aligned with the process of discipleship. You can't have rogue staff members leading parts of the church in a direction contrary to the rest of the congregation.

Simple is Wise Stewardship

The economic landscape in America has changed dramatically since the release of *Simple Church*. At the time of writing this additional chapter, few people would attempt to argue that we are out of the current economic downturn. While the financial forecasts vary, most agree that our current generation will forever be marked by the "new economy."

Some churches have been required to make significant cuts during the economic downturn. Due to growth, the value of stewardship deeply implanted in the church, or the region of the country being less impacted by the economy, others churches have maintained their giving patterns throughout the rough economy. Regardless of the context, the "new economy" should impact thinking about church finances.

With potentially fewer resources, churches must finance what is absolutely essential. For the essential to be excellent, the non-essential may need to be starved.

Churches committed to a simple process for discipleship are enabled for wise stewardship because they are committed to only funding what is essential to their mission. Complex churches tend to be very fat; they tend to finance multiple directions, programs that are inward, ministries that do not add much value, and fluff.

Donors in the "new economy" will become more discretionary in their giving, as they desire to know exactly how their gifts will advance the kingdom or make an immediate impact. Churches that demonstrate wise stewardship will build credibility with donors as they are committed to stewarding resources for the biggest impact.

Bottom-line: complex is more expensive than simple.

Simple Creates Space for Missional

Dell Computers has shattered the warehouse myth. Most companies love big warehouses. They feel safe with lots of inventory on big shelves in big warehouses, always ready for the next big order. They feel as if they will always be able to meet customer demands and customer expectations. Dell disagrees. They do not want their resources on the shelves. In the technology business, the product loses value on the shelves. So Dell only keeps two hours of inventory. Two hours! Which means that if you order a PC on dell.com, the parts will not arrive to Dell until two hours before your PC is shipped to you.

Dell wants their resources out there, on the street, not in the warehouse. So Dell has designed a very strategic process to move their best resources out of the warehouse as quickly as possible.

Sadly, many churches still believe in the warehouse myth. They build big warehouses and shelve a bunch of Christians. They keep them in the warehouse with an onslaught of weekly programs.

A simple process moves a church's greatest resource (the people) to the street where they can be salt and light in their context. Because of frequent questions on the relationship between "simple" and "missional" Eric and Ed Stetzer wrote an article entitled "Simply Missional," where they explored the relationship. They wrote:

Is there a relationship between a church being missional and a church being simple? While we have not done quantitative research with hard data, we have made some qualitative observations. Churches who are living as missional communities in their culture are often quite simple. In the same way, churches that are designed around a simple process are embracing the call to be missionaries in their culture. The relationship between being missional and being simple is apparent for at least six reasons.

First, being missional and being simple requires strategic thinking. Thinking strategically is not isolated to one aspect of church leadership. The type of leaders who think strategically about how to best reach the community around them are the same type of leaders who think strategically about their church programming and process.

Second, living a missional life is a part of a simple discipleship process. Many churches believe discipleship equates information transfer. This faulty premise assumes that the only thing lacking is that church folk do not know enough. So when one of these churches seeks to ramp up their "discipleship," they typically look to add another type of curriculum or Bible study structure. These churches produce a bunch of Bible study junkies who sit in the warehouse with yet another workbook. Churches with a simple process have a broader definition for discipleship. They seek to lead people to be doers of the word, not just hearers (James 1:22). They seek to move people to a place of living a missional life. Discipleship to these churches is not information, but transformation. And a true disciple is someone who seeks to transform the community around him. A disciple understands he is a missionary. These churches streamline their programming to create space in the lives of their people to live as a disciple/missionary in their community.

Third, simple churches offer less at the church building thus creating opportunities for missional living. We continually have listened to the moans of church leaders. We have heard the cries from pastors for years, "our people just do not seem to know lost people."

Hmmmm. Perhaps our church people do not know lost people because our churches have kept people at the church building, thereby nullifying their opportunities to deeply engage in relationships with lost people. Leaders often guilt people into coming to the church, removing them from the world. Churches with minimal programming help their people live among the world as missionaries by not asking them to live at the church, but to live as the church.

Fourth, missional and simple leaders know the culture. Missional leaders love the city or town in which God has placed them. They exegete the culture by embracing and embedding themselves in it. They do not study it from a distance but they know people, real people who are far from God. Leaders in simple churches are afforded the awesome opportunity to know the culture from the inside out.

Fifth, both missional and simple are people-focused, not program-focused. Missional churches give thoughtful consideration to the community in which God has placed them. They view their resources and their programs as tools for people's lives to be transformed, and they train their members to think this way. In fact, this is a significant portion of the discipleship process, or program. Simple churches view their programs the same way. As tools. Their programs are slaves to the discipleship process God has given them. Their programs or environments are tools that God may use to produce life change.[3]

As you read this, *Dell's* parts were being moved to the street. Out of the warehouse. What about the people in your church? They are your greatest resource. Are they being distributed to the world around them? Do you have a simple process to move them to missional involvement?

And when it's all said and done, that last question may be the most important. Does the simple process truly lead to the making of disciples? If it doesn't, it's an utter failure.

Thank you for your making *Simple Church* a much-discussed book these past five years. And thanks for hearing from us five years later. But now it's time to put the book down, and get back to the missional task of making disciples. That's what really matters.

It's really that simple.

Research Design Methodology

After our continual observation that vibrant churches are much simpler than struggling churches, we committed to research this hypothesis. We sought to explore the relationship between church vitality and a simple church design. The research design consisted of three steps: survey development, sample identification, and data collection.

Step 1: Survey Development

We could have chosen the case study method of research and chronicled the impact of vibrant and vital churches that have a simple process. Our observations of simple churches have been numerous and have taken place over several years. The case study approach would have been valid and acceptable research. However, we would have been unable to make broad research implications and applications. Researchers call this "limits of generalization." The more limited the research is, the less applications may be made for those outside the research population.

Instead, we decided to include hundreds of churches in the research project from a broad research population. By involving hundreds of churches in the project, we would be able to make sound recommendations to the entire church world based on the research findings. We desired for the research to be as objective as possible, so we worked to develop a survey that would measure the simple process design of a church. The use of a survey brings more objectivity to the research than just interviews. Interviews alone allow the subjectivity of the interviewer to enter the research equation.

We developed the survey (Process Design Survey) based on the four simple church elements we observed in simple churches: clarity, movement, alignment, and focus. The Process Design Survey also measures how strongly a local church excels in each of the four key elements. We assembled an expert panel to develop the survey. The panel consisted of seasoned and experienced church leaders. On the panel were denominational leaders, pastors, ministers of education, church planters, and seminary professors. The panel chose which items would be on the survey and reached consensus on the wording of those items.

The Process Design Survey was then put through a rigorous field-testing process. Church leaders from within the sample population completed the survey in order to discover the validity and reliability of the survey. The Chronbach Alpha Index of internal consistency on the survey is a .97. A 1.0 is perfect, and most researchers feel confident using a survey that has a Chronbach Index of .80.

Step 2: Sample Identification

The research was conducted in two phases. In both phases, random stratified sampling was used to identify the churches that would be surveyed. Stratified sampling involves seg-menting a sample from a research population into two or more subgroups. We chose to divide the potential population (churches) into two strata: a vibrant/growing church strata and a comparison/nongrowing church strata.

In stratified sampling, the subgroups/strata are identified through parameters given by the researchers. In both phases the parameters we used to identify both strata were the same. The vibrant/growing churches were churches that grew in worship service attendance a minimum of 5 percent a year for three consecutive years. This is at least 15 percent growth over a three-year period. Unfortunately, few churches experi-ence this kind of growth. In fact, our research indicates that less than 2 percent of all churches in the United States experi-ence this type of growth. The comparison/nongrowing strata in both phases of the research were churches that had grown less than 1 percent over the same three-year period. These were churches that had not grown or had declined.

Our sampling was also random. After the strata parameters were set, churches that fit into both strata were randomly selected to participate in the research project. In phase one of the research, the Market Research and Intelligence Department at LifeWay Christian Resources provided us with a random list of the churches based on the accurate data they keep on local churches. In phase two of the research, the Rainer Research Group (Thom's previous work) provided a random list of churches based on their data.

In the first phase, four hundred churches from each strata were identified. The churches surveyed in phase one were all Southern Baptist churches. Many researchers believe that in the initial phases of church research, one denomination should be used so that easy comparisons may be made. In other words, the researcher is comparing apples to apples. We chose to use Southern Baptist churches in the first phase for several reasons. First, the Southern Baptist Convention (SBC) is the largest denomination in the United States and would allow us to interact with as many church leaders as possible. Second, the size of the SBC would allow us to survey churches from varying geographical and cultural settings. Third, the SBC believes highly in the autonomy of the local church. In other words, each church in the SBC is free to structure and operate as it deems best. So while some churches in the SBC may choose to use a simple church design, others may choose not to do so. This would give us some great insight into the impacts of a simple church design.

In the second phase, one hundred churches from each strata were identified. The churches surveyed in phase two of the research included a broader representation from the evangelical church world. Nondenominational churches and many evangelical denominations participated in phase two of the research.

As always the case in research, not every church participated in the project. In phase one, there were 166 participating churches from the vibrant/growing strata and 153 from the comparison church strata. In the second phase, there were 44 participating churches from the vibrant/growing strata and 44 from the comparison church strata. Overall, 208 churches from the vibrant strata participated while 197 churches from the comparison church strata participated in the project.

Step 3: Data Collection

We contracted with EDCOT© (www.edcot.com), an educational research company, to format the Process Design Survey in an online format. EDCOT© built two survey Web sites for the data collection. One Web site was designed for the vibrant church leaders and another for the comparison church leaders. By having two distinct survey Web sites, we were easily able to compare information between the two strata. We developed a third temporary Web site where respondents could go for free consulting based on their responses. When a respondent completed the survey, the respondent received a score and a link to the free consulting Web site. This was used to increase the level of candor and honesty of those completing the survey.

We assembled a team of people to call each church in the random stratified sample. The team asked for the pastor of the church. The pastor was told about the appropriate Web site based on his church's strata and about the free consulting he would receive if he completed the survey. During this phone call, we also attempted to secure the e-mail address of the senior pastor.

We then followed up with a letter to the senior pastors in both strata. Several days later, we sent an e-mail to the pastors of whom we had addresses. In most cases, the senior pastor completed the survey. However, other staff completed the survey at times. We instructed the pastor to pass on the survey to a senior staff member if he had delegated the responsibility of the process to another leader.

Throughout the data collection process, we had countless conversations with church leaders about the simple process at their church. We heard stories about the focus of the vibrant churches, and we heard stories about the struggles of the complex churches. We learned a lot.

EDCOT© stored the data in two separate databases. After the survey was closed, we gave the data to a statistical consultant, Dr. Paulette Johnson at Florida International University. Our statistical consultant interpreted the data through a myriad of statistical tests including inferential tests known as *t* tests and ANVOA testing. Significance was found at the .001 level on all of these tests for both the entire survey and for each simple church element. The difference in statistical terms for the first phase of research is as follows:

According to the data there is a highly significant relationship between a simple church design and the vitality of a local church, $t(317) = 7.36$, $p < .001$.

According to the data, there is a highly significant relationship between clarity and the vitality of a local church, $t(317) = 6.84$, $p < .001$.

According to the data, there is a highly significant relationship between movement and the vitality of a local church, $t(317) = 7.64$, $p < .001$.

According to the data, there is a highly significant relationship between alignment and the vitality of a local church, $t(317) = 6.26$, $p < .001$.

According to the data, there is a highly significant relationship between focus and the vitality of a local church, $t(317) = 6.31$, $p < .001$.

APPENDIX B

Frequently Asked Questions

Q: Are you suggesting that a simple church design will cause a church to be vibrant?

No. Ultimately it is God who brings growth and vitality to a local church. Also, it is against the laws of research to assert causation. We cannot claim that a simple church design causes anything. We are simply saying that there is a relationship between a simple church design and the vitality of a local church. And this relationship is highly significant.

Q: Aren't there other factors related to the vitality of a local church?

Of course there are other factors, but it would be impossible to measure all of the factors in one research study. The study would become inconclusive because too many variables would be included in the research. However, we did include a few demographical questions in the survey to test the strength of the simple church design. We used ANOVA testing to control against the demographical items. The relationship between a simple church design and the vitality of a local church remained highly significant at the .001 level.

Q: How did you choose the parameters for each strata?

We initially set the requirements for the vibrant/growing church strata too high at 10 percent growth a year for three consecutive years. Of the forty-three thousand churches in the Southern Baptist Convention, fewer than two hundred met that requirement. Sadly, we had to lower the bar so that we would have enough churches to do extensive research. The parameters for the vibrant/growing church strata were set at 5 percent growth a year for three consecutive years. The antithesis of this is a stagnant church. Unfortunately, the vast majority of churches meet this parameter. An equal number of churches from each strata were randomly selected for the research project.

Q: Why did you choose worship attendance as a measure of the growth of the church?

Church growth/vitality is not only about attracting people. It is about attaching them to others and to a place of ministry. It is about life transformation. Research indicates that people only remain in worship services over time as they are moved to greater levels of commitment. Measuring the church's annual average weekly worship attendance measures the ability of the church to attach people, not just attract them. Many churches may be able to lead people to Christ, but then fail to assimilate them into the life of the church.

Q: Who completed the survey for each church?

While churches comprised the sample, church leaders were surveyed as representatives of the church. The most appropriate person to survey and interview for the church is the leader of the church's discipleship process. In most cases, this is the senior pastor. In some cases, the senior pastor has delegated this responsibility to an executive or associate pastor. In our research we allowed the "owner" of the process to complete the survey.

Q: Were all major denominations included in the study?

Yes, in the second phase. In phase one of the study, we focused solely on Southern Baptist churches. In phase two, we invited churches from every major evangelical denomination to participate in the study.

Q: Did you limit the study to churches in the United States?

We did for the issue of "generalization of findings." We wanted to make applications based on the findings, and that would be hard to do as the nature of ministry changes so much as international borders are crossed. However, we do feel that many of the concepts may be applied internationally. We have conducted the survey with a group of church leaders in El Savador and found an overwhelming response. Unfortunately, churches in other countries are influenced by our programming here in the United States. We pray that churches on international soil will not mimic the complexity of the American church.

Q: How did you reduce the impact of your bias?

Obviously we had bias going into this project as we had observed the impact simple churches were having. To reduce the influence of our bias, we worked with an expert panel to develop an objective survey. The Process Design Survey was tested for internal consistency and provided us with objective data.

Q: Do you have any concerns about how church leaders will respond to the challenge?

Yes. We are concerned some may move too quickly. We are concerned because we hear over and over again how frustrated church leaders are with the complexity that is leading to no life change. We pray leaders will follow the Spirit's leadership and implement change with wisdom and compassion.

Q: I am not the senior pastor. What can I do?

First, you must be sure you are under the authority and the leadership of your senior pastor. If you have the freedom to implement a ministry design for an area of ministry that you lead, then design a simple discipleship process for your ministry area that has clarity, movement, alignment, and focus. Perhaps God will use the new simplicity and focus in the department you lead to change the culture of the entire church.

If you would like to take the Process Design Survey that was used in the research phase of Simple Church, you may do so at www.ericgeiger.com.

After completing the survey, you will be given a score along with feedback based on your responses. This will help you evaluate your church's process and prepare to make necessary changes.

Notes

Chapter One

1. Keith Hammond, "How Google Grows and Grows," *Fast Company* 69 (April 2003), 74.

2. Steven Heller and Anne Fink, *Less Is More: The New Simplicity in Graphic Design* (Cincinnati, Ohio: North Light Books, 1999), 25.

3. Jack Trout and Steven Rivkin, *The Power of Simplicity* (New York: McGraw-Hill, 1999), 186.

4. Ibid.

5. Steven M. Cristol and Peter Sealey, *Simplicity Marketing: End Brand Complexity, Clutter, and Confusion* (New York: The Free Press, 2000).

6. Arthur Agatston, *The South Beach Diet* (New York: Rodale Books, 2003), 7.

7. John MacArthur, *Matthew 19–23* (Chicago, Ill.: Moody Press, 1988), 337–38.

8. Eric Reed and Collin Hansen, "How Pastors Rate as Leaders," *Leadership Journal* 24, no. 4 (Fall 2003), 30.

Chapter Four

1. Andy Stanley, *Foyer to the Kitchen: Is What Is Hanging on the Wall Happening Down the Hall?* Video cassette produced by Northpoint Community Church.

2. Andy Stanley, Reggie Joiner, and Lane Jones, *Practice Number 1: Narrow the Focus*. From the Seven Practices of Effective Ministry series posted online at www.practically speaking.org.

3. Andy Stanley, Reggie Joiner, and Lane Jones, *Seven Practices of Effective Ministry* (Sisters, Oreg.: Multnomah, 2004), 92.

4. Ibid., 89.

5. Stanley, *Foyer to the Kitchen*.

6. Andy Stanley, Reggie Joiner, and Lane Jones, *Practice Number 2: Think Steps Not Programs*. From the Seven Practices of Effective Ministry series posted online at www.practical lyspeaking.org.

7. Stanley, Joiner, and Jones, *Seven Practices of Effective Ministry*, 105.

Chapter Five

1. Thom S. Rainer, *Surprising Insights from the Unchurched and Proven Ways to Reach Them* (Grand Rapids, Mich.: Zondervan Publishing House, 2001), 122.

2. Michael Hammer, *Beyond Reengineering: How the Process-Centered Organization Is Changing Our Work and Our Lives* (New York: Harper Business, 1996), 14.

3. Michael Hammer, *The Agenda: What Every Business Must Do to Dominate the Decade* (New York: Three Rivers Press, 2001), 101–24.

4. Michael Hammer and S. Stanton, *The Reengineering Revolution: A Handbook* (New York: Harper Collins Publishers, 1995), 48.

5. Interviewed by Kevin Miller and Richard Doebler, "Visionary Jazz: An Interview with Max Depree," *Leadership Journal* (Summer 1994), 17–23.

Chapter Six

1. Thom S. Rainer, *Surprising Insights from the Unchurched and Proven Ways to Reach Them* (Grand Rapids, Mich.: Zondervan Publishing House, 2001), 120.

2. Ibid., 188.

3. Ibid., 114.

Chapter Seven

1. Max Depree, *Leading without Power: Finding Hope in Serving Community* (Holland, Mich.: Shepherd Foundation, 1997), 32.

2. Paul Hersey, Kenneth H. Blanchard, and Dewey E. Johnson, *Management of Organizational Behavior: Utilizing Human Resources*, 7th ed. (Upper Saddle River, N.J.: Prentice Hall Inc., 1996), 158.

3. Jack Welch, *Winning* (New York: Harper Business, 2005).

Chapter Eight

1. S. Anderson, *Brain*, vol. 128 (January 2005), 201–12. News Release from the University of Iowa.

2. Linda Tischler, "Google's Secret Weapon," *Fast Company* 100 (November 2005), 56.

3. Ibid., 56.

4. Travis H. Bradshaw, "Evangelistic Churches: Geographic, Demographic, and Marketing Variables That Facilitate Their Growth," Ph.D. diss., University of Florida, 2001.

5. Michael Jordan, *Driven from Within*, ed. by Mark Vancil (New York: Atria Books, 2005).

6. Linda Tischler, "Google's Secret Weapon," 54.

7. Walter Mossberg, *The Wall Street Journal*, 14 June 2004, B1 as quoted in *"The One Thing You Need to Know,"* by Marcus Buckingham (New York: Free Press, 2005), 165.

8. Steven M. Cristol and Peter Sealey, *Simplicity Marketing: End Brand Complexity, Clutter, and Confusion* (New York: The Free Press, 2000), 246.

9. Jack Trout and Steven Rivkin, *The Power of Simplicity* (New York: McGraw-Hill, 1999), 8.

10. Jack Welch, *Winning* (New York: Harper Business, 2005), 170.

Chapter Nine

1. Thom S. Rainer, *The Bridger Generation* (Nashville, Tenn.: Broadman & Holman Publishers, 1997).

2. Alan Deutschman, "Change or Die," *Fast Company* 94 (May 2005), 54–62.

3. Tom Peters, *The Circle of Innovation* (New York: Random House, 1997), 37.

The Postscript

1. Vince Poscente, *The Age of Speed: Learning to Thrive in a More-faster-now World* (Austin, Tex.: Bard Press, 2008).

2. John Kotter, *Leading Change* (Boston Mass: Harvard Business School Press 1996).

3. Ed Stetzer and Eric Geiger, "Simply Missional," *Neue* Quarterly, Fall 2008.

About the Authors

Thom S. Rainer, Ph.D., is the president and CEO of LifeWay Christian Resources, one of the largest Christian resource companies in the world. He has consulted with more than five hundred churches, served as pastor in four churches and interim pastor in seven churches, and spoken in hundreds of venues. His publications include more than twenty books and hundreds of articles. He and his wife, Nellie Jo, have three grown sons: Sam, Art, and Jess, are proud grandparents, and live in Nashville, Tennessee.

Eric Geiger serves as one of the vice presidents at LifeWay Christian Resources, leading the Resources Division. He received his doctorate in leadership and church ministry from Southern Seminary. Eric authored or coauthored several books including *Transformational Groups*.

Eric is married to Kaye, and they have two daughters: Eden and Evie. During his free time, Eric enjoys dating his wife, playing with his daughters, and shooting basketball.

Researching To Reach A Rapidly Changing Culture

To reach your neighborhood, your community, your city, you need to know it inside out. Our Church Leadership Library resources are based on a sweeping commitment to understanding cultural trends based on real data. Through state-of-the-art research tools, we are listening to churches, we are listening to Christians, and most of all we are listening to the lost – so that you can build your ministry not on the world as it was, but as it is and will be. With these resources, you are holding tomorrow's tools in your hands today. To learn more about the church leadership tools of tomorrow, visit ChurchLeadershipBooks.com.

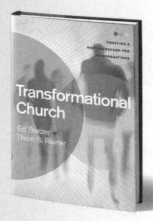

Creating A New Scorecard for Congregations

The Younger UnChurched And The Churches That Reach Them

Reclaiming A Generation of Dropouts

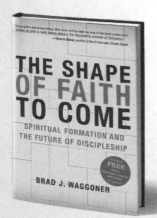

Spiritual Formation And The Future Of Discipleship

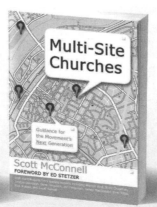

Guidance For The Movement's Next Generation

Books Powered by

Archived studies can be found at LifeWayResearch.com.

ChurchLeadershipBooks.com